MW00581168

BEAUTY BY THE SEASONS

Grow, Gather, and Heal with
Wisdom from Our Ancestors

More than 100 Plant-Based Recipes

By Conya J. Gilmore

Copyright © 2021 by Conya J. Gilmore

All rights reserved. No part of this book may be reproduced or transmitted in any form or by any means, electronic or mechanical, including photocopying, recording, or by any information storage and retrieval system, without written permission from the author.

FIRST EDITION

Note: This publication contains the opinions and ideas of its author. It is intended to provide helpful and informative material on the subject matter covered. It is sold with the understanding that the author is not engaged in rendering professional services in the book. If the reader requires personal assistance or advice, a competent professional should be consulted.

The author specifically disclaims any responsibility for any liability, loss or risk, personal or otherwise, which is incurred as a consequence, directly or indirectly, of the use and application of any of the contents of this book.

First printing edition *2021.*

Printed in the United States of America

In Memory of My Grandparents

Granddaddy Edward who showed me the beauty and strength in being present in the moment...and to ignore questions already answered.

~

Grandma Ethel who showed me the joy found in discovering the perfect nail polish for Saturday Nights and to never shrink myself for anyone or anything.

~

Granddaddy Tillman who showed me how to birth new dreams and actualize new paths.

~

Grandma Geraldine who showed me that we carry generations on these hips and move through mountains with our love, joy and buttered rolls.

~

Mama Lily who showed me the art, healing, wisdsom and value in our gathering.

Love & Gratitude,
Conya

CONTENTS

Introduction

**If Beauty is our Intention.
Time and At(intention) must follow.**

As a kid I loved being outside; climbing trees, making mud pies, chasing butterflies, and eating tomato's straight off the vine as I trailed behind my Grandma in the garden. These are snapshots in time that shaped how I experienced beauty in the natural world and within people.

This book grows out of my experiences living and growing up in rural SW Virginia, observations, stories, apprenticeships, studies, and conversations with women in my family and community. Over the decades we have preserved our traditions with each generation; evolving our beauty rituals into our own.

Watching my family and community define beauty, wellness and healing on their own terms laid the foundation for this book as a celebration of old and new traditions. I've gathered recipes passed down to me from Elders throughout the Blue Ridge Mountains. and my travels around the world to bring together a collection of recipes for self-care and intentional beauty in a time of (re) evolution.

I feel we heal ourselves and our communities when we are intentional with our time, compassionate with our thoughts, attentive to our personal beauty rituals and spiritual healing.

I am my best work - A series of Road Maps, Reports, Recipes, Doodles and Prayers from the Front Lines.

~

Audre Lorde

Taking the time to make our own beauty rituals is not a new thing. Somewhere along the journey of time we forgot that all beauty products don't have to come in a package. Whether it is drinking a calming tea, spritzing a refreshing hydrosol, releasing the day with an herbal bath, massaging worry filled tension away with healing oils they all lead us along the pathway to reconnecting with the earth's energy around us. Gifting ourselves with the time to absorb the healing from herbal hair rinses or teas to ease anxiety is part of our inheritance.

I'm excited and grateful for the opportunity to share a few stories, recipes and ride along on the journey to reclaiming our time.

The abundance throughout these pages are possible with the gifts of our relationship with Water, Air, Earth, Fire, and Spirit. This book is divided into the four seasons, which cover beauty from a place rooted in the energy of the natural world around us and the guidance of our Ancestors.

You will find some traditional recipes as well as my adaptations from my own healing travels. You will also find similar receipes with different methods of preparation. Try different methods and apply what works best for you.

There is always something to do. There are hungry people to feed, naked people to clothe, sick people to comfort and make well. And while I don't expect you to save the world, I do think it's not asking much for you to love those with whom you sleep, share the happiness of those whom you call friend, encourage those among you who are visionary and remove from your life those who offer you depression, despair and disrespect.

~

Nikki Giovanni

OUR GRANDPARENTS GARDEN

When we look at our parents, we see that behind them are their parents, and behind their parents are their parents, and continuing on generation after generation.

This same life force, love and resilience flows through all of them until it reaches us.

My hope is to add to the conversation a record that gives thanks to our ancestors whom faced many struggles and highlight their joy, passions, and love that they passed down generation after generation. So when our grandchildren's grandchildren look through their family tree they will know us not just by our names or struggles but the love we passed through the roots that continuously nourish them.

They will know us by our joy of picking the perfect tomato right off the vine while walking through the garden for a mid-morning snack.

They will know us by our joy of chasing lightning bugs and june bugs on cool summer nights, the card games we play long into the late hours of the night during holidays, the healing in our gathering for family reunions and homegoings.

They will know us through the ever present laughter woven into our stories, the handwritten notes peppered throughout family recipe books, cakes and cobblers baked for birthdays and church revivals, the music and dances we enjoy to release or hold a little tighter to a moment.

They will know us by the muscle memory passed down through the generations of snapping beans, shucking corn while sharing the latest bit of family gossip, and eating fresh steamed crab straight in from the shore on summer nights full of laughter, full bellies, and impossibly clear star laden skies.

Our children will know that their ancestors passed to them more than land and knowledge of working with the land but a deep residing well of empowered self-love. A love from within that grows our capacity to release our overflow to nourish others.

It is my hope that while reading some stories along with the recipes that it encourages you to find the space in your life to honor and create memories with your familial group and community.

"How simple a thing it seems to me that to know ourselves as we are, we must know our mothers' names."

Alice Walker

The history of African Americans in this country is a lengthy one that begins virtually at the time of exploration.

Our often hyphenated name, in all of its complexity, hints at the intricate mixings of our past. We are a race that never before existed: a cobbled-together admixture of Africa, Europe, and the Americas. We are like no others before us or after us.

Involuntarily taken from a homeland, molded in the crucible of enslavement, forged in the fire of disenfranchisement, and tempered by migration, we all too often remain strangers in the only land that is ours. Despite all this, we have created a culinary tradition that has marked the food of this country more than any other.

-Jessica B. Harris, Culinary Historian and Author

How to Use this Book

Beauty by the Seasons is divided up by the four seasons with recipes celebrating the use of fresh and dried ingredients while taking advantage of each season's energy. The book includes tips on how to start your own beauty garden, harvest, dry and preserve herbs; methods for infusing plant medicine into your daily beauty routines with each season, fun ways to use elixirs and syrups for everything from cocktails to mini pound cakes; tips on planting your own windowsill, kitchen or backyard garden.

The intention for **Beauty by the Seasons** is to provide an easy, relatable, interesting, informative and fun resource. It contains quotes, poems, rambling thoughts and stories from my life.

This book is based on my experiences growing up in SW Virginia and travels around the world. You'll notice that mixed in with body, face and hair recipes you will find delicious champagne gummies, cake's, cocktails, ice cream and more in each season. You don't have to read the book cover to cover. You may want to start with the season you're in or the season you are approaching to lay the groundwork and prepare for upcoming needs. You can continue adding recipes to your routine each new season as you go through the year. But, for those looking for a deep dive into changing how they center themselves in their own life then I recommend that you read from front to back straight through. Make notes and make a plan to grow some, all or as many of the plants that you can (see section for Growing a Beauty Garden). You can also buy most ingredients from a local herbal apothecary, farmers market or CSA.

Working with plants (that you grow and harvest) seasonally gives your mind the connection to the energy of the season and your body the nutrients it needs. As we change seasons we do not have to make large sweeping changes; many plants crossover two to three seasons. Generally, I like to maintain my skin-care ritual throughout the year with adaptations as we move through the changes of each season. Our bodies know for example, that on a hot summer day we are usually not reaching for a hot stew or a heavy meal but a fresh salad filled with dandelion greens and ripe tomatoes. Your skin as well will appreciate a spritz from a hydrosol or body toner in the summer and will thankfully soak in nourishment from a healing body butter during dry cold winter months.

I hope you enjoy this work, find places of connection, alignment, practices that strengthen your resiliency, and bring you joy!

Beauty by The Seasons
Grow, Gather & Heal

SETTING UP A
BEAUTY APOTHECARY

Create a personal creative self care space something that works for you.

Starter Essentials
My top 5 that I always have everywhere I go. Beauty has no border limitations.

Labels
Measuring cups and Measuring spoons
Metal and plastic strainer
Storage containers with lids for your body products
These can include: glass jars, plastic ice cream containers, canning/mason jars, glass dropper bottles, glass spray bottles.
- Jars: All sizes. Start with 2, 4, and 8 oz glass jars with lids.
- Bottles: 2 and 4oz amber or blue glass dropper and spray bottles for elixirs, syrups, tinctures, extracts and hydrosols.

Teapot
I find I'm much more likely to drink tea regularly when I use a cute teapot. These small aspects can turn a (recipe) into a sweet ritual for yourself. I also have a french press just for herbal teas. I often use it to prepare overnight infusions and quickly strain them in the morning.

Home Beauty Apothecary
In addition to the above...

Blender or Food Processor

Cheesecloth

Double boiler or a Glass bowl

Funnels of various sizes

Grater or Mortar and Pestle

Small, Medium and Large Glass or Ceramic Mixing Bowls

Ice Cream Maker

Knives

Small, Medium, and Large Size Saucepan

Spoons

Spatula

PLANT ~ GROW ~HARVEST

Growing a Beauty Garden

GROWING A BEAUTY GARDEN

On the following pages many of the plants listed will be easy to find or simply grow yourself. Try growing a plant or two or three on a sunny window sill or back deck if you're just starting out. If you already have a garden give yourself a lil challenge and grow something new. Also, if you choose to harvest your herbs from the "wild", a process known as wild crafting, be mindful and conscious to the following practices: Identify your herbs, harvest from a safe location and take only what you need.

Many of the plants used for medicine by our grandparents have been over harvested and are now endangered. There is a worldwide shortage of medicinal plants; it is important that we are conscious in our responsibility to know the production journey of our plants. As a community we must make every effort not to use plants that are endangered, at risk, or harvested unethically.

A few questions to ask when buying herbs
Where do the herbs come from?
Who is growing them?
Who and how were they harvested?
Are they organically grown?

Why Grow Your Own Beauty Garden

Growing a beauty garden is a unique part of gardening that can be immensely satisfying in amplifying your self care routines.

There are many benefits of growing your own plants but here are a few to think about:

- Knowledge: you will know where they come from and under what conditions they were grown.
- Access: you will have easy and consistent access to fresh and dried plants
- Quality: you will be able to control the quality and use the best to fill your cup

WHERE TO PLANT

Outdoor: Window boxes, raised beds, vertical stacking containers and ground containers.

Indoor: Window sill boxes, containers, pots, and planters of varying sizes.

What will work best for your garden space?
Where do you want it to be?

Indoor gardens are great opportunities if you are trying gardening for the first time or have a small space.

Outdoor gardens are great when you have room to spread out. Decide what you want to grow, pick a spot, and sketch out your garden design.

Container Gardens: Repeat of growing indoors. Great option. Outside there is a little more flexibility because you can move plants to where they will grow well and be safe if a location is not working out.

Container Gardens: Containers let you take advantage of wherever you have sunshine. Driveway, backyard, roof, patio, or window boxes. Smaller containers are good for getting an early start. For deep rooted plants you'll need 5 gallon or deeper containers. Get creative, especially with repurposed items. Whatever you choose, it needs to drain. Punch holes in the bottom and you're set.

It is very important to keep your container garden watered. For people that are often on the go then self-watering containers are great. They do well if you have a window or patio that receives about 6 hours of light for your herbs. Also, allows easy access to all of your plants. so that if you want a cup of lemon balm tea you do not have to go far.

Balcony Tips
- Watering is a priority. Note, do you have a south or west facing balcony. Does your balcony get windy?
- Great option for many small balconies or decks is vertical gardening. Stack planters, railing planters, vertical wall planters and hanging baskets for a beautiful and functional garden.
- Wind shear. Essential to consider the direction and the amount of wind shear your balcony receives especially the higher the floor level.

Raised Bed Gardens: Using a raised bed is a great way to control the type of soil you are using, keeping plants organized and weeds under control. There are many advantages to a raised bed.

- The soil drains well and warms up faster in the spring.
- You can frame your raised beds with lumber or other materials, such as bricks or stones.
- A framed border of some sort is attractive, prevents foot traffic, and defines your beds.

Observe your space and decide the width and length you want your bed to be.

In-Ground Garden: Working directly in the soil can be very successful by preparing the land and planting in the ground.

I do a mixture. I have plants like mint, lemon balm, and aloe that I grow indoors. I have outdoor containers, raised beds and in-ground garden space filled with herbs and vegetables.

What To Grow in your Garden? Dream, brainstorm and make a list.

What do you love? Taste, Smell, Feel?
What herbs do you know you love?
What medicinal benefits would you like to have by using plants?

Now that you have these ideas written down think about if you want to plant in the spring, fall, winter or all year round. For example, rosemary can be grown all year round in a small container in your kitchen.

Herbs and vegetables can be annuals, biennials, or perennials.

- Annuals are plants that germinate, bloom, produce, seed, and die, within one year. These include many flowers, herbs, and vegetables. Calendula is an example of an annual herb.
- Biennials have a two-year biological cycle. They grow leaves the first year, and flower, seed, and die in the second year. Beets are an example of a biennial plant.
- Perennials are plants that live on for several years. They can flower or fruit year after year. Lemon Balm is an example of a perennial herbs.

How to Start Your Own Beauty Garden

We can grow herbs from seeds, cuttings, or existing plants.

- Many herbs like calendula are easy to grow from seeds but not all.
- Some herbs are easy to propagate from cuttings, such as lavender, than from seed.
- Existing plants are often ready to be harvested. This allows you to cut and use some of the stems or leaves while leaving most of the plant to continue growing.

Sunlight
Sunlight is the fuel for your plant growth. If you want to grow a variety of plants, you need at least six to eight hours of sunlight every day between spring and fall equinoxes. Observe the area for your future garden, note the quality (full or partial sun) and the amount of sun you will have. And while, yes, enough sunlight is crucial, too much sunlight and heat in late summer can be brutal. During these hottest months my okra and watermelon thrive.

Starting your seeds:
There are various ways to grow healthy herbs in your beauty garden. Refer to the instructions on the seed packets that you are using. I start my seeds in starter cells or eggshells.

What about Soil?
Read the instructions on the seed packets for the best soil recommendations for what you are planting. Many herbs need well-draining moist soil to do well in a garden. Depending on the type of herb will determine if you need more alkaline (basic) or acidic soil. The only way to know what type of soil you have is to use a soil tester to check the pH of your soil. Except for sunlight and carbon dioxide, plants get everything they need from the soil.

I also like to work in a fresh layer of compost to the soil to give it much-needed nutrients. Composting is a great way to give your herbs the nourishment it needs. You can also use organic soil treatments to add nutrients for your seedlings if you don't have access to compost.

Water
Adequate moisture is essential for healthy plant growth. Plants need water to carry nutrients and keep their tissues hydrated. Even short dry periods can stunt plant growth, reducing your yields dramatically.

A few watering tips:

- Check plant needs before waterings. Water according to need. A set schedule may not always work especially when growing in containers.
- Water at the right time of the day. Watering at night or early in the morning, avoiding the hottest part of the day, reduces water loss (and diseases as well.)
- Watering cans. It's a good idea to have at least two sturdy watering cans. I like 1 or 2 gallon light weight metal or plastic cans for gently watering new transplants and helping sensitive plants through a dry spell. Make a little circle in the soil like a saucer around the plants before you sprinkle, so the water soaks into the root zone instead of running off.

Personal Note
Reminder: It's your garden. Do what you want. Love on it and let it love on you.

I begin my mornings during this time with a cup of herbal coffee while watering my plants. I learned from my Great Grandma Lucy that everything living wants love and attention. So, I talk to my plants about any and everything, play music (from speakers placed throughout the garden) varying from the Rock, Funk, Soul Goddess Betty Davis to the versatile and melodic Rhiannon Giddens, poetry from Maya Angelou or Sonia Sanchez, speeches and interviews from James Baldwin or Paul Robeson, and Jill Scott's podcast. Love me some *J.ill the Podcast*.

Transferring Your Seedlings:
Transfer your seedling's when they have at least two levels of leaves. Refer to the seed packet and seller's guide for more detailed information for planting and transfer time table.

Harvesting Your Herbs
Most of the herbs fall into these categories: leafy, woody-stemmed, or flowering. With this comes different ways to harvest these herbs to best suit your beauty apothecary.

Leafy:
Herbal Examples: mint and lemon balm
Gather what you need, as you move through the growing season. You do this by picking the leaves off. The only thing that I would encourage you to do though is pick from the outside in. This will tell your plant to grow more. Use fresh or dried.

Woody-Stemmed:
Herbal Examples: rosemary and thyme
Gather from the outside in and cut the whole stem from the bottom. To use this herb you can use it fresh or dried, and remove the herbs from the whole stem. The stem can then be composted.

Flowering Herbs:
Herbal Examples: lavender and chamomile
Pick what you need and use the flower heads dried or fresh.

Storing Herbs:
Herbs retain their properties best if stored in an airtight glass jar, away from direct light, in a cool storage area. Each herb has its own "shelf life" or duration of time in which it remains viable. Use the standards of quality look, taste, and smell to determine if your herbs are still good. The medicinal properties of dried herbs degrade the longer they sit. This degradation occurs even faster when the herbs are exposed to light. Avoid storing herbs in plastic bags because they will take on the properties of the plastic.

Buying Herbs:
We are allies of plants. Make every effort to not use a plant on the endangered list. Use a substitute. I'm repeating the questions below because during the time this book is published, 2021, most people who live in the United States of America have access to purchase most fresh or dried herbs from anywhere around the world. With that privilege comes responsibility of knowing and asking the questions of whether "we should or do we need to". This is not for me to decide for you but more so a part of your healing and connective journey to our cousins around the world. What is the accessibility of our cousins in other parts of the country or world? Some of my thoughts and questions to ask when buying herbs.
- Buy from reputable apothecaries, farms, and gardens.
- Ask questions:
    - Where do you get your herbs?
    - How are they harvested?
    - Who harvests them?

Using Your Herbs:
As you will read in the following pages plant medicine is a part of my everyday life. It's important to choose healing herbs that are appropriate for your body, skin and hair type. Infusing a menstruum with herbs is an easy process that doesn't take much time.

Fresh or dried herbs? When in season and where possible I prefer fresh. However, with a few exceptions, all of the recipes in this book use dried herbs (so that you can use them even if you are not growing the plant yourself).

DRYING METHODS

You can use the herbs fresh from your garden but also dry them to use throughout the year. Timing is everything when it comes to drying herbs. They should be picked before the flowers develop and harvest on warm, dry mornings after the dew has evaporated. Because each herb grows differently, I recommend picking and preparing one variety at a time.

DRYING METHODS

No matter which drying method you choose, effective drying relies on abundant dry, fresh air more than heat. A well ventilated place out of direct sunlight. The process might be slower if you live in a humid area. In that case mold could be a problem so I recommend using a small commercial dehydrator.

Air Drying

Option #1: Hanging. To hang dry herbs, tie sprigs or branches into small bunches. *Hang the bunches up to dry, leaves downward, wrapped loosely in muslin or thin paper bags to keep out dust and to catch falling leaves or seeds. Avoid using plastic bags because of mold development.

Allow seven to ten days to dry, depending on the size of the branches and humidity.

*Large, dense bunches can develop mold and discolored leaves.

Options #2: Rack Drying. You can speed up drying by spacing out individual sprigs or leaves of herbs on racks. To make a drying rack, stretch muslin, cheesecloth or netting over a wooden frame and fix it in place. Place the tray in an airing cupboard, in the warming drawer of an oven or in a warm, airy spot out of direct sunlight. Turn leaves frequently to ensure even drying, which should take two or three days.

Both of the air-drying methods will take approximately one week to dry, depending on the the amount of humidity where you are. The more moisture in the air, the longer it will take. A simple crumble test can determine if they are ready. If you take a leaf in your palm and crush it, does it come apart easy? If so, you're ready to store.

Dehydrating

A home dehydrator is a great way to dry herbs in large quantity. Make sure the leaves are clean and undamaged and then put them in a single layer on each tray. Set on the lowest setting. Follow directions given in your machines manual for timing. for approximately two to four hours.

Oven Drying

Space leaves out out on a muslin-covered tray in an oven set to the lowest possible temperature with the door ajar to allow moisture to escape. Turn the leaves over after 30 minutes to ensure even drying; they will be quite dry within an hour. Leave in the oven until cool.

How to Store Dried Herbs

To store herbs, crumble the dried herbs with your fingers and store in small, airtight containers. Discard the hard leafstalks and midribs.

PLANTS
I
LOVE

SMELL THE ROSES

In this chapter, I discuss some of my favorite herbs that I grew up with and some that I have learned to grow over the years. They have all become mainstays in my life.

Note: The Importance of Latin Names. I've included a Latin and a common name for each herb. Herbalists use Latin names to avoid confusion over the identity of a plant. Many plants share common names which can differ from place to place (region to region), but each plant has only one Latin name.

It is recommended that you consult with a healthcare practitioner before using herbal products, particularly if you are pregnant, nursing, or on any medications.

Aloe (*Aloe Vera or A. Barbadensis*)
Zones: Zones 8 to 11; Full/Part Sun. Perennial

Fleshy leaves that produce a juice from their leaves can be used to relieve pain from scrapes and burns when applied topically. Aloe produces new leaves from its center, so if you are obtaining sap, cut the outermost and oldest leaves first. One of the best herbs for soothing skin and healing burns, rashes, and frostbite. It is also used to treat eczema, dandruff, acne, ringworm, gum disease and poison oak and ivy. We often use in creams and lotions for softening and moisturizing skin.

Blackberry (*Rubus sp.*)
Zones: 6 to 8; Full/Part Sun. Perennial
Dark green leaves; mature berries are firm and black to purple-blue color/fruit.

Blackberries, plucked straight from the vine, are one of my favorite Summer highlights. To make a great, tea, though look to the leaves. Although the flavor is mild (and a little sweet), the leaves contain antioxidants, vitamin C, E & tannins. Harvest them in the morning or evening when temperatures are cooler, You can use both fresh and dried leaves in tea. The high antioxidant content of blackberries are known for lowering cholesterol and reducing the risk of cardiovasculoar disease; the berries are also high in vitamin C, calcium, potassium, and magnesium.

Chamomile German (*Matricaria recutita*)
Zones: 2 to 8; Annual. Full Sun.
Yellow center and white petals, bloom from June through August. Grows up to 2 feet tall. For optimal growth, do not over water.

Bitter, Sedative, Relaxant, Nervine, Anti-inflammation, Anti-histamine, and Tonic. An anti-inflammatory to reduce swelling and infection; an antispasmodic to relieve digestive upsets, headaches, menstrual cramps; calm nerves, and cleansing wounds. Used in creams and lotions to soothe sensitive and irritated skin, treat rashes and skin allergies. Used on bruises, sprains, and varicose veins and almost any time th skin becomes inflamed. Its calming action induces sleep, and relieves nervous indigestion.

Comfrey (*Symphytum officinale*)
Zones: 3 to 9; Full Sun to Partial Shade. Perennial.
A hardy, leafy plant that dies down in winter and comes back in the spring. Various species have purple-pink flowers and appear from May through the first frost.

Astringent, Demulcent, Nutritive, Tonic, and Emollient. Used for bruises, wounds, and sores. Used in creams, salves, and baths to soothe, soften skin and promotes growth of new cells. Heals & protects damaged tissue throughout the body. Aids in soothing inflammation and when used as a poultice can be applied to sore breast, burns, wounds and swelling & bites.

Dandelion (*Taraxacum official*)
Zones: 2 to 10; Full Sun. Perennial. Yellow flowers that top hollow stems. Flowers appear in mid-spring and close at night. Dark green leaves are jagged and grow close to the ground in a rosette with deep roots.

Hepatic, Nutritive, Digestive Stimulant, Astringent, Sedative, Diuretic, Tonic, Bitter, and Alterative. Leaves are rich in minerals and vitamins, vitamin A, B2, C and K and calcium. Dandelion root's diuretic properties may help lower blood pressure and relieve premenstrual fluid retention. Unlike most diuretics, it retains potassium rather than flushing it from the body. Great for soothing the nervous system, helping with sleep and stress related digestive issues.

Ginger (*Zingiber officinale*)
Zones: 9-12; Full Sun to Partial Shade. Perennial.
Ginger Root: tan colored roots with green stalk.

Anti-inflammatory, Anti-spasmodic, Aromatic, Nervine, Stimulant, Tonic, and Anti-viral. Rich in vitamins B6 and B5, potassium, manganese, copper and magnesium. A stomach calming aid, reduces gas, bloating and indigestion and aids in the body's absorption of nutrients and other herbs. Used internally and topically. Stimulates circulation, so if you are cold, you can use warm ginger tea to help raise your body heat.

Lavender (*Lavandula anguvstifolia*)
Zones: 5-8; Mint family, Perennial
Bushy plant with silver gray, narrow leaves. 1 1/2 to 2-foot flower stalks topped by fragrant purple-blue flower clusters. Flowers in June and July. Full sun. Harvest flowers when they are in late bud stage, just before they bloom.

Anti-inflammatory, Anti-bacterial, Anti-depressant, Sedative, Stimulant, and Tonic. Excellent skin healer: Promotes healing of burns, abrasions, infected sores, other types of inflammations, including varicose. Used for sore muscles in massage oil, relieves lung and sinus congestion. Excellent compress for a headache, sore eyes, or skin injury. Dynamic herb great for relaxation or mental stimulation.

Lemon Balm (*Melissa officinalis*)
Zones: 3 to 7; Partial Sun to Shade. Perennial
Low-growing herb grows about 18-24" high; often used as ground cover. Bees love the white and yellow flowers that bloom from June to August. Regular pruning during the growing season helps keep it from going to seed or spreading to fast.

Nervine, Anti-depressant, Anti-microbial, and Anti-viral. Lemon Scent and citrus flavor but a member of the mint family. Flavor is light; recipes featuring lemon balm often call for lemon juice too, because the herb is too mild to pack a lemony punch. Mild, minty flavor. Used to reduce stress, anxiety and to promote sleep.

Oatstraw (*Avena sativa*)
Zones: 2-11; Full Sun. Annual.
Grass crop growing to 4ft tall and 8"-1ft wide. Can be planted in the fall or early spring for maturity in the summer or fall. They are direct seeded in place in the garden in rows.

Anti-depressant, Nutritive Emollient, Diuretic, and Demulcent. Nutritive-dense herb that soothes the nervous system. Stabilizes your blood sugar levels, any nervous constitutions, Insomnia, feeling under nourished, low libido, constipation, rebuild the myelin sheets around your nerves, grief, and trauma. Oats are an annual crop good choice for the permaculture garden. It prevent soil erosion making it an excellent cover crop.

Red Raspberry (*Rubus idaeus*)
Zones: 4-9; Full Sun. Perennials.
Leaves are made up of 3 to 5 oval leaflets with serrated margins and light gray, hairy undersides. Grow up to 6 feet.

Alterative, Anti-spasmodic, Astringent, Stimulant, and Tonic. Great sources of potassium and iron. Low in calories but high in fiber, vitamins, minerals and antioxidants. Strengthens the female reproductive system. Used to strengthen and invigorate the uterus, increase milk flow, and restore the mother's system after childbirth.

Rose (rosa, spp)
Zones: 7-10; Full Sun. Perennial.
There are over a hundred species and thousands of cultivars. They can be erect shrubs, climbing or trailing, with stems that often have thorns.

Anti-depressant, Anti-spasmodic, Astringent, Anti-viral, Anti-inflammatory, Digestive stimulant, and Sedative. Contains vitamins and antioxidants that can help soothe and repair the skin. It also offers astringent properties, making it an excellent combatant ofacne, redness, and inflammation. It is a cleansing, loving herb; great for releasing grief and womb or heart related trauma.

Rosemary (*Rosmarinus officinalis*)
Zones: 7 to 9; Full Sun. Perennial.
a shrub with fragrant, evergreen, needle-like leaves and white, pink, purple, or blue flowers.

Anti-bacterial, Anti-fungal, Anti-microbial, and Anti-septic. Rich source of antioxidants and anti-inflammatory compounds. Used to help alleviate muscle pain, improve memory, boost the immune and circulatory system, and promote hair growth. Rosemary helps to increase scalp circulation by more oxygen and nutrients being sent to your hair follicles. This promotes healthy hair growth while treating dandruff, itchiness and scalp irritation.

Skullcap (*Scutellaria lateriflora*)
Zones: 5-8; Partial Shade to Full Sun. Perennial.
Square stems and the jagged edges of its leaves. tube-like, violet-blue flowers of Skullcap bloom from June to September.

Nervine. Tonic, Anti-spasmodic, Sedative, Anti-bacterial, Aromatic, Astringent, and Diuretic. Used for insomnia, anxiety, ptsd, and trauma. It is also used for allergies, skin infections, inflammation, and spasms. Soothing and calming herb used in baths and salves to ease tension, reduce stress and calm down the nervous system.

Stinging Nettle (*Urtica dioica*)
Zones: 3 to 10; Full Sun to Partial Shade. Perennial. Can grow up to 4 ft in ideal conditions. Grow it containers and prune often. The underside of the leaves are covered in small hairs (trichomes). The small hairs are sharp, so it's best to wear gloves, long pants and long sleeves when planting and harvesting stinging nettle.

Histamine, Diuretic, Tonic, Alterative, Nutritive and Anti-inflammatory. Leaves are eccellent sources of vitamins A, C and K; several B vitamins; beta-carotene; calcium, cooper; iron; magnesium; and potassium. Used for allergies, muscle aches, urinary tract infections, and inflammatory diseases.

SECTION 3

RECLAIMING OUR
HEALING
TRADITIONS AS
WE MOVE
INTO THE FUTURE

RECLAIM THE FUTURE

My earliest memories are of me and my cousins running through the woods, splashing in creeks, eating blackberries, making mud pies and rainbows with our Grandparents garden hose. There was so much beauty, peace in these moments...in the rhythm of sunrises filtering through our Grandma's yellow and green curtains. The early pre-dawn sounds of my Granddad moving about the house and lighting all the fires for the different wood burning stoves throughout the house. Life revolved around being fully present in each moment and it was easier to just breathe. To settle into oneself and receive the medicine that comes from hearing the space between sounds, smelling honeysuckles through the weeds, and truth telling with wild dandelions dancing at your feet. How do we hold onto and carry this piece of peace into this next evolution of the modern world? For me and mine it will be through love of self, family and community.

Generations of Ancestor wisdom stretches into our kitchens, churches, farms, bbq joints on back country roads, barber shops, and hair salons to bring us the sweetness of self-care for the experiences to come.

This book continues the legacy passed down through the generations of my Black farming community and the wisdom of living in union with the seasons. There is magic in growing, eating, and living according to the season that you're in. The recipes in this book create a roadmap to maintaining our joy, health, and right mind through old and new traditions. We honor, preserve and build upon medicine and wisdom passed to us from our Elders. As we stay rooted in in our foundation we stay flexible to the winds of change. Our medicine must reflect our new and changing realities and environments. Reimaging what working in community, growing and harvesting plants as medicine for those that come after us.

Our Ancestors endured through generations of pain, trauma and oppression to find ways to pass on to us their joy, resilience, and wisdom as we move through the seasons. They come in the forms of family lore, recipes, hymns, plant medicine, laughter, prayers, and wisdom about everything in between. As we go forward and continue paving the way for the next generation it is up to us to extend our hands back and accept their wisdom.

This is the time to pour into ourselves and reclaim growing, harvesting, sharing and using traditional and new plant medicine practices. Letting ritual ground us to the present moment, relaxing into it, and preparing our soil to dream + manifest our destiny. A rhythm that connects our physical and emotional spirit with nature growing and hibernating around us. Let the natural order of life cycles ground you and guide you in this journey. Choose to create moments that bring you joy and nourish your skin, hair, body and spirit.

Eat well, slowly. Use plants as your Allies.
Remember that we are connected to everything; past, present and future.
Stay consciously in the moment. Breathe, Hydrate, Sleep and Rest.

To acknowledge our ancestors means we are aware that we did not make ourselves, that the line stretches all the way back, perhaps to God, or Gods. We remember them because it is an easy thing to forget; that we are not the first to suffer, rebel, fight, love and die. The grace with which we embrace life, in spite of the pain, the sorrows, is always a measure of what has gone before.

Alice Walker

The Seasons: Attuning Ourselves to Earth's Cycles

Spring: CROWN
Spring is a time of purpose...purposeful creation of self-care habits to set the energetic tone for the year.

I am a Spring baby and use this season to center and align my mind and body as the season thaws from the winter cold into the cool breezes of Springtime. Allow yourself this time to create sacred spaces that you can go to often throughout the year. A place that you feel safe and at peace. It can be as simple as a closet (upper room vibes), spare bedroom, a spot in your garden, or a favorite window seat. A place where you can go for one or thirty minutes to focus on your breathing, connect to the energy beneath your feet and experience being in that moment.

Use this time to (re)imagine and dream what ritual looks and feels like to you. Play. Let the renewed energy of Spring flow through your CROWN and root you to the soil.

Summer: HYDRATE
Imagine...Color, Organic and Locally Grown. Putting the care of self into the summer light makes these moments a ritual that you maintain throughout your life. Whether it is growing your own food or buying fresh ingredients from local farms. Use this time to create and align with rituals for your life. You reflect and create beauty in your own way.

Ritual
A sequence of activities involving movement/gestures, words, actions, or objects, performed according to a set sequence. Rituals may be prescribed by the traditions of a community.

As the season's harvest is continuous during this season, buy from local farmers directly, at a farmers market or through a CSA. Let the colors of the season inspire you. Eat colorfully, organic and local. Enjoy the variety of colors, taste, smells and versatility of food eaten in season.

Hydrate...water is your best friend all year round but especially in the Summer months. It is easy to get dehydrated. When you start feeling thirsty it is already too late and you are already on your way to being tired, depleted, and dehydrated. Water, Water, Water.

One of my clearest memories from my childhood is my Grandaddy and his water jug. My Granddaddy Edward kept a jug of water with a glass in the fridge that he would drink from throughout the day. Whenever we would ask our Grandparents for something to drink, the answer was always "Drink water". I can smile and laugh at that now but at the time "I was not amused". Although, as a kid this was not the answer I wanted to hear, it nonetheless has served me well as I've unconsciously carried the message into adulthood. Water is now my favorite drink of choice. Well to be more exact throughout the day I actually drink room temperature water with a healthy squeeze of lemon lime. However, like many of you I also enjoy a good cup of coffee in the morning or a glass of wine in the evening but the key is balance and moderation. If you drink coffee, alcohol or wine follow up with a glass of water.

Fall: NOURISHMENT
Let the rhythm of the seasonal change guide and nourish you.

Whether it's a five mile run, yoga in the park, a walk around the neighborhood, a hike in the mountains, a 30 minute bike ride or a 15 minute dance party to The Labelle's, *Lady Marmalade*, find time to get movement in every day. And sweat! Sweating is good for your skin in releasing toxins. We are more relaxed, eat better, sleep consistently and breathe deeper when we get consistent movement and exercise in our lives..

Use this time to ready your soil and soul for what is ahead. Take comfort in nature's reminder that rest for the earth's soil and for our own soul is essential. Notice what gives you energy, nourishes you and move into that flow intentionally.

Winter: BODY & SOUL
Restoration and Sanctuary during the Winter months.

Pause. Step fully into the moment and pause. Like the land, we need rest...nurturing and restorative rest for our bodies and mind. Use this time to rest and restore within your sacred space. Rest and sleep are priorities during this time. Every part of your life...mind, body and soul suffers when we don't get enough rest.

Create a bedtime ritual to signal to your body it is time to release the day. Try drinking a calming tea, applying a soothing balm or relaxing room spray. Add practices that build upon these moments to move forward with intention and gratitude.

Find comfort in nature's reminder that rest, as good as it is for the soil, is good for the soul too.

Cleanse. Rest. Hydrate. Protect. Nourish. Restoration. Repeat.

As I finish editing this book I am spending the month with my two year old niece, Sweet Baby Cheeks also known as Lucy, and my original intention for writing this book has never felt more true and imperfectly perfect.

I am passing down our family traditions and love to her in a myriad of quiet ways. We have our daily rituals of walking through the garden, talking to our plants, watering, caring for them and harvesting. She has a little toddler size watering can, gardening hat and apron to carry her little tools and spray bottle. Just today, mid-morning we picked some peppermint for our afternoon iced tea. We placed them in the jar and I turned away for just a moment (that's all it takes with a toddler...lol) when I turned back around only to find that she's mixing them in different buckets of water and mud pie pans just as happily as she could be. My first inward thought was "Oh, no! That was for our tea!" But just as that thought came it was replaced with the realization or perhaps the remembrance that our medicine is deeply rooted but ever growing. She knows what she's doing, what she needs...muscle memory of generations of healers are whispering and teaching her. I am but one voice. I can and will pass to her what has been passed to me but just as I have dreamt and lived new realities from those of my ancestors she will grow up in a world that her generation will shape and steer, not mine. I can prepare her with this foundation but she will continue to shape this medicine into what will be needed in the world she will be a part of guiding.

It is our honor. It is our legacy.

SECTION 4

PURPOSE

SPRING

CREATING HABIT

RECLAIM THE FUTURE

Wash Day Joy...

Sweet Tea, Blue Magic & Beaded Braids

Saturday Afternoons. Ritual
Tears. Laughter. Hours and Hours.
Array of combs, brushes, blue magic and sweet tea.
Front porch, warm breezes, lemonade & endless beads.

HIBISCUS AND HONEY CO-WASH

LAVENDER AND OATS CO-WASH

SPRING CLEARING HERBAL HAIR RINSE

DEEP CONDITIONING HAIR MASK

FEELING GOOD DAY & NIGHT CONDITIONER

TWIST & BRAIDS HAIR MIST

MO' BETTER CURLS, COILS, & TWIST BUTTER BALM

HERBAL HAIR OIL INFUSION

LEMON LIME WATER

SO BERRY SMOOTHIE

HIBISCUS, LAVENDER & ROSE TEA

TEA TIME
~
WHO ALL OVER THERE? MARTINI
MAMA LILY'S SWEET TEA

BLACKBERRY & ROSE POPSICLES

HONEYSUCKLE ELIXER

HONEYSUCKLE POUND CAKE

BLACKBERRY COMPOTE

HIBISCUS BALM HYDRATING SPRAY

JASMINE FACE & BODY MIST

MA' DEAR'S FACIAL STEAM

LILAC TONER

CLEOPATRA JONES MILK BATH

JASMINE ALOE SHOWER GEL

MAGNOLIA BODY BUTTER

JASMINE MASSAGE OIL

SUN SOOTHER BALM

HIBISCUS & HONEY
CO-WASH

A good co-wash is a way to nourish and cleanse your hair without using traditional shampoos. An effective co-wash will leave your scalp feeling clean, hydrated, and moisturized. The goal is to both wash and condition your hair. While balancing hydrating and cleansing your coils.

INGREDIENTS

1 tbsp hibiscus flowers
1 tbsp raw honey
1 tbsp argan oil
1 tsp coconut oil
1 cup distilled water

EQUIPMENT

measuring spoons and cups
2 small bowls
hand mixer or blender
strainer
spoon

PREPARATION

Add hibiscus flowers and one cup of hot water to a medium size bowl. Let steep for 15-20 minutes. While the hibiscus is steeping, add honey, argan oil, and coconut oil in a 2nd bowl. Mix by hand or use a blender.

Strain hibiscus flowers and compost. Pour the hibiscus tea into the 2nd bowl. Blend together well. Set to the side. Let cool before using.

TO USE

This mixture should be cool enough to use, but test with your fingers before applying to your hair. Using a blender will loosen the honey so it can maneuver through curls and coils with ease. Apply on wet hair and let sit for five to ten minutes. Rinse well.

DID YOU KNOW...?

Distilling your own water is simple. Heat your tap water to the point that it turns to vapor. When the vapor condenses back to water, it leaves behind any mineral residue. The resulting condensed liquid is distilled water.

LAVENDER AND OAT
CO-WASH

Light and Nourishing...Lavender nourishes and stimulates hair growth while the oats leaves behind softness and shine keeping your hair moisturized, shiny and coils frizz free.

INGREDIENTS

2 tbsp lavender flowers
1 1/2 tbsp plain oatmeal
2 cups organic coconut milk
1 tbsp unrefined coconut oil

PREPARATION

Heat coconut milk, lavender and oatmeal at a low simmer for three minutes. Remove from heat and let steep for 1-2 minutes. Strain. Compost the oats and lavender.

Add coconut oil to the herbal infused coconut milk. Stir thoroughly until mixed well. Set to the side. Let cool before using.

TO USE

This mixture should be cool enough to use, but test with your fingers before applying to your hair. Apply on damp or wet hair and let sit for five to ten minutes. Rinse well.

DID YOU KNOW...?

Co-wash stands for "conditioner-only hair washing," which involves relying solely on conditioner, and not shampoo, to keep hair moisturized, prevent frizzy curls, and avoid the dreaded dryness shampoo brings.

HERBAL HAIR RINSE

Cleansing and Clearing. Spring is the perfect time to release what was and embrace what is. Embracing and moving forward with new beginnings that come naturally with the cycle into the Spring Season. Nettles. rosemary, and comfrey work to help in stabilizing, grounding, and adding mental clarity while protecting you as this new season unfolds.

INGREDIENTS

2 tbsp rosemary
1 tbsp nettles
1 tbsp comfrey
6 cups distilled water

EQUIPMENT

1 quart jar with lid or heat proof container with lid
medium saucepan or pot
cheesecloth
small bowl or measuring cup
measuring spoons

PREPARATION

Add rosemary, nettles, and comfrey in a quart jar. Pour hot water over the herbs and fill to the top. Close with lid and steep from 30 minutes to overnight.

Strain the herbal infusion using the cheesecloth. You may need to strain it two or more times to get all the plant mater out. If some sediment remains after you've strained don't worry about it. If you are not using right away then label and refrerate to keep longer.

USE

Cleanse and rinse your hair as you normally do. Then pour the rinse over your head and massage into your scalp.

Rosemary is a great all-purpose herb that you can grow indoors and outside. Used to stimulate and improve circulation to the scalp; encouraging hair growth. It's high antibacterial quality allows it to gently cleanses and increase the shine to your hair.

How to Give Your Scalp a Massage

Starting at your forehead. Using the fingertips of both hands, lightly apply pressure at the center of your forehead. Release it after a few seconds. Continue by moving your fingers slowly up onto your scalp. Continue applying pressure then releasing from the front to the base of your scalp at the back of your head.

Next, continue to move your hands farther apart so that there's about an inch of space between the fingertips of each. Continue applying pressure then releasing it from the back to the front of your scalp.

Then move your fingers even farther apart so that there are 2 to 3 inches of space between the fingertips. Continue these movements spreading the fingers farther apart each time you reach the front or back of the scalp until the entire scalp has been massaged.

DEEP CONDITIONING
HAIR MASK

Celebrating our resilience and that ever soothing feeling of a deep conditioner. I swear I can feel my scalp and hair follicles breathing a deep "Ahhhhhhhhh". Block off your calendar, put your phone on mute and enjoy a few chapters in that book you've "been meaning to read".

INGREDIENTS

3 tbsp comfrey
1 tsp cornstarch
2 tsp flaxseed
1 tbsp honey
1/2 cup coconut milk
4 oz grapeseed oil

EQUIPMENT

stainless steel saucepan
stainless steel double boiler
glass measuring cup
bowl
cheescloth
glass jar with lid
wide mouth jar with lid

DID YOU KNOW...?

Flaxseeds are rich in vitamin E, which is great for both skin and hair health. The nutrient promotes the health of the scalp by reducing free radical damage. It helps improve circulation in the head, thus promoting hair growth and slowing down hair breakage.

PREPARATION

Double Boiler Herbal Oil Infusion
Place a stainless steel saucepan on the stove, filling it ¼ full of water, and bringing the water to a steaming simmer. Keep on low heat.

Add grapeseed oil, comfrey, and flaxseed into a second double boiler pan. Use a spoon to mix thoroughly and no air bubbles. Stir.

Place the smaller, herbal mixture filled saucepan inside the larger, water-filled saucepan and simmer for 2-3 hours, keeping a careful eye on the amount of water in the larger saucepan and being very careful not to let water splash into the herbal mixture. If the water level runs low in the lower saucepan, carefully add more hot water to bring the water level in the saucepan back up to ¼ full.

When the infusion process is finished, using cheesecloth, carefully strain all the plant matter from the the oil. Transfer the oil to a glass bottle or jar with a lid. Label and date the container. Store in a cool dark place.

USE
Pour Comfrey Flaxeed oil infusion into a bowl. Mix in coconut milk, cornstarch, and honey. Blend well. Apply to clean hair. Leave in for 30-45 minutes. Rinse well. Store leftover in refrigerator.

DAY & NIGHT CONDITIONER

This conditioner combines three natural beauty mainstays for some serious deep conditioning. Jojoba oil adds moisture and softness, argan oil helps control frizz, and shea butter remedies split ends while soothing dry scalps.

INGREDIENTS

2 tbsp lavender infused jojoba oil
1 tbsp shea butter
1 tsp argan butter

EQUIPMENT

double boiler or small heat-safe glass bowl
small saucepan
measuring spoons
spoon
whisk
shower cap
2 oz glass container with top

PREPARATION

Using a Glass Bowl

Combine shea and argan butters in a small heat-safe glass bowl. Stir, mix well.

Bring two inches of water to a boil in a small saucepan, then reduce the heat to low. Place the glass bow inside the saucepan and melt the oils together.

Remove the bowl from the heat, let cool for between 3-5 minutes, and add the jojoba oil. Stir to mix well.

Refrigerate the mixture until it starts to set, approximately 20 minutes. Whisk until it's frothy and easy to apply.

USE

Using your fingers work into the scalp from front to the back. Then comb the mask through clean, hair and cover with a shower cap. Leave on for 30-60 minutes, then rinse your hair and style as usual. Store any leftovers in a container with a lid. Use 1 to 2 times per month.

HAIR MIST

INGREDIENTS

1/2 cup distilled water
1/2 cup aloe vera juice
2 1/2 tsp vegetable glycerine
1 tbsp avocado oil
1 tbsp castor oil
3-4 drops of essential oil
2-3 drops of tea tree oil

EQUIPMENT

2 -4 oz or 1 -8 oz spray botte

PREPARATION

Add aloe vera juice, glycerine, avocado oil, castor oil, tea tree and essential oil into spray bottle. Shake.

Add the distilled water to the oil mixture. Shake well.

USE

Spritz lightly on scalp and braids as needed.

Recommend making small amounts and keeping in the refrigerator to extend the life of the spray. It will be good for 4-6 weeks.

Pick your essential oil

Peppermint:
Promotes the health of hair follicles. Instantly refreshing scent.

Rosemary:
Calms, promotes hair health, relieves dry scalp.

Cedarwood:
Calms, relieves itchiness and dandruff. A scalp soother. Works well with rosemary for healthy hair tonic.

Bergamot:
Stimulates the scalp and strengthens hair. Mixes well with jasmine and rosemary.

Distilled water is used to increase the life span of the spray and to ensure there is no bacteria or any other unwanted substances.

Aloe vera promotes hair growth, gets rid of frizziness and helps to get rid of dandruff.

Glycerine keeps your hair moisturised as it can absorb humidity from the air. In addition, glycerine also strengthens your hair and aids in growth.

Avocado oil helps to heal heat damaged hair and also add shine to hair and prevents hair loss.

Castor oil seals in moisture keeping hair hydrated, helps to treat split ends, promotes hair growth and revitalises dry scalp.

The tea tree oil help to sooth the scalp and to prevent dandruff.

BUTTER BALM

INGREDIENTS

1/4 cup hibiscus flowers
1/2 cup jojoba oil
1/4 cup coconut oil
1 tsp almond oil
1/2 cup argan butter
10 drops tea tree oil
1/2 cup distilled water

EQUIPMENT

glass measuring cup
small and medium funnel
blender
8oz glass jar with lid
wide mouth jar with lid
double boiler (optional)
spoon or silicone spatula

PREPARATION

Part 1
Sun Herbal Oil Infusion

Place hibiscus flowers in a jar. Pour jojoba oil covering plant material to the top of the jar leaving 1/8 to 1/4" space at the top. Close with lid. Label with contents and date. Place in the sun for infusion. Strain 4-6 weeks later. If you don't have time for a sun infusion then use the double boiler or stove infusion method.

Part 2

Combine water and hibiscus infused jojoba oil, almond oil, coconut oil, and argan butter into a double boiler; warm over low heat. Pour the oils into the blender or standing bowl for hand blender. Let cool to room temperature. The mixture will become thick and creamy with a white color.

After the mixture has cooled then turn on the blender at medium to high speed. Slowly pour water in the middle while blending. Watch the cream consistency closely and turn off the blender when the mixture looks thick like cake frosting. With a hand spoon or silicone spatula continue stirring and add the drops of tea tree oil. Slowly mix in more water if needed but do not over stir. The cream will thicken as it sets.

Spoon the mixture into glass wide mouth jars. Store in a cool location. They do not need to be refrigerated.

USE

Apply on wet or dry hair as you style or braid. For protective styles, use to seal the hair with moisture before styling. For locs, apply cream as you retwist each strand for shine, definition and hold.

*The water must be at room temperture and the oils must be completely cool. If the water and oils separate, then start over.

HERBAL HAIR
OIL INFUSION

This is a shout out to all the hair oils that saved the life of my hair and announced my entry into any room with the scent of earth, soil, and sun-filled sweetness.

INGREDIENTS
4 oz jojoba oil
2 tbsp lavender
1 tbsp nettles
1 tsp rosemary
15 drops patchouli essential oil
2-3 drops tea tree

EQUIPMENT
4 oz glass jar with lid
measuring spoons
small and medium funnel
2 -2oz or 4oz glass bottle with eye dropper

Patchouli has a rich woody and musky scent that reminds me of the endless braid styles I've worn over the years.

It is an antiseptic, astringent, and fungicide making it excellent for healing scalp conditions.

Patchouli's antidepressant, sedative, and aphrodisiac properties soothe and restore the mind.

PREPARATION
Sun Herbal Oil Infusion
Place lavender, nettles, and rosemary in a jar. Pour jojoba oil covering plant material to the top of the jar leaving 1/8 to 1/4" space at the top. Close with lid. Label with contents and date.

Place in the sun for infusion. Strain 4 weeks later. If you don't have time for a sun infusion then use the double boiler or stove infusion method.

Add herbal infused oil, tea tree, and cedarwood essential oil into glass eye dropper bottles. Use funnel to pour oil into glass bottles. Add label with contents, date, and usage on the bottle.

USE
A little goes a long way! Apply a few drops to the palm of your hand and work the oil evenly into your hair. Can be used on wet or dry hair for added moisture either on its own or with other hair balms.

As a scalp treatment, apply a few drops to targeted areas around your head. Massage oil into the scalp.

SO BERRY
SMOOTHIE

One of my many Springtime joys is berry picking with my sister Courtney. There is no sweeter berry than the one you've picked yourself under a hot late Spring sun. This smoothie reminds me to seize the moment and that berries are at their peak ripeness and ready for harvest. Even better, freeze them and enjoy all summer long. You can try it with all 4 ore just one or two!

INGREDIENTS

1/4 cup blackberries
1/4 cup raspberries
1/4 cup blueberries
1/2 cup strawberries
1/4 cup spinach
1 tbsp peanut or almond butter
2 tbsp flax seed, ground
3/4 cup water or oat milk(or milk option of choice)

PREPARATION

Add all ingredients into blender.

Pulse until smooth. Enjoy.

Yield: 1 serving

DID YOU KNOW...?

Leafy greens like spinach are rich sources of folate, a natural form of vitamin B9 with antidepressant properties. Folate plays a key role in the synthesis of serotonin and dopamine which are two of our "happy brain chemicals" known to boost mood and concentration.

GRAN'MERE LIZ'S
TEA HOUSE

INGREDIENTS

Cocktails
3/4 cup hibiscus flowers
1/2 cup lavender flowers
1/2 cup rose petals
1 lemon
2 cups sugar
1 -750ml bottle vodka
2 cups water
ice

Herbal Tea
2 tbsp rooibos
2 cups water

EQUIPMENT
glass bowl with lid
3 - 8 oz glass jars with lid
strainer

PREPARATION

Part 1
Add 1/2 cup hibiscus flowers to an 8 oz jar. Fill the jar with vodka.

Gently muddle the flower petals about 5-6 times. You just want them to start releasing some of their flavor. The vodka will become bright pink within minutes, but it will take longer for the flavor to infuse in the vodka. Infuse for 2-3 hours. If the flowers steep for longer than a few hours, the vodka may become bitter.

Decant, strain and bottle in a jar with lid. Label jar with contents and date.

Part 2
Hibiscus: Cold infusion. Steep 2 tbsp hibiscus in 8 oz of water at room temperature in an overnight.

Lavender and Rose: Mix lavender, rose and sugar into a glass bowl. Stir in 2 cups of hot water and mix evenly. Cover the bowl and rest overnight.

The next day, continue with making the simple syrup. In a saucepan, add water on medium heat until it begins to steam. Reduce temperature to low when the water and slowly stir in the herbal sugar mixture. Stir until all of the sugar dissolves. Remove the herbal syrup from heat, strain, and pour into a glass jar. Let cool.

MAMA LILY'S SWEET TEA
WHO ALL OVER THERE? MARTINI

My Grandma Mama Lily's Herbal Sweet Tea: Steep 1 tbsp of rooibos in 1 cup of hot water for 20-25 minutes. Strain and add Lavender Rose syrup or honey to your taste. Refrigerate until chilled and ready to use.

MAMA LILY'S SWEET TEA

- Fill cocktail glass with ice.

- Squeeze in the juice of half a lemon.

- Add 1 1/2 oz vodka

- Add 4 oz herbal sweet tea and stir.

- Garnish with lemon; if desired.

WHO ALL OVER THERE? MARTINI

- Fill cocktail shaker with ice.

- Add 2oz hibiscus infused vodka

- Add 1 oz lavender and rose syrup.

- Shake vigorously for 10-15 seconds until the shaker is well-chilled.

- Strain into chilled martini glasses.

- Garnish with lemon curl or lavender spring if desired.

LEMON LIME
WATER

Hydrate all year long. Water has always been how I begin and end my days.
Lemons and limes are full of vitamin C with cleasning and antioxidant powers.
It's calming effects in the digestive system relieve, bloating and heartburn.

INGREDIENTS

3 lemons
2 limes
water
ice, optional

EQUIPMENT

32 oz glass pitcher or container
knife

**Did You
Know:**
Cucumber is usually considered a
vegetable because of how it's used in
the culinary world. However, as it
grows from flowers and contains
seeds, it's botanically a fruit.

PREPARATION

Squeeze lemons and limes into a glass
pitcher. Fill with cool to room temperature
water.

Enjoy at room temperature or add ice for
desired temperature.

Yield: 32 oz

This recipe also works well for
fruit...try it with fresh picked
strawberries or cucumbers.

HIBISCUS, LAVENDER
AND ROSE TEA

This tea reminds me of my Great Grandmother Lucy's flawless skin that felt like it never aged. Her rose bush would bloom every year with the most beautiful rose petals that were used for the perfect early morning tea. Over the years I added hibiscus and lavender to create a powerful nourishing skin tonic that makes space for a grateful heart and a peaceful mind.

INGREDIENTS

2 tsp hibiscus flowers
1 1/2 tsp rose petals
1/2 tsp lavender buds
1/4 tsp fresh ginger root; grated
1 1/2 cups water
honey; sweeten to taste
lemon; optional

Equipment
measuring spoons and cups
spoon
tea kettle or saucepan
strainer

PREPARATION

Add hibiscus, lavender, rose and ginger to strainer and place in tea pot.

Pour hot water through the herb filled strainer into the tea pot.

Steep tea for 20-25 minutes. Strain, add lemon juice and sweeten as desired.

Yield: 1 serving

BLACKBERRY & ROSE
POPSICLES

I love all types of ice treats. Popsicles, ice cream, and slushies all fill me with joy. I love making them and creating new recipes. It's a simple thing but sometimes it's the simple things that bring us the most joy. Give this recipe a try. The combination of vitamin packed blackberries and soothing roses are perfect for sun-filled afternoons.

INGREDIENTS

4 cups blackberries
1 cup red raspberries
1 tbsp rose petals
8 tbsp sugar
2 tbsp lemon juice
1 tbsp ginger, grated
1 tsp rosewater
1 cup water

Equipment

small saucepan or pot
spoon
strainer or sieve
food processor
pitcher
popsicle molds
wooden sticks
ladle

PREPARATION

Part 1

Make Simple Syrup:
In a small saucepan over medium-high heat, bring roses, sugar and 1 cup of water to a simmer. Stir until sugar dissolves. Set aside until cool, about 10-15 minutes. Strain.

Part 2

Purée blackberries and red raspberries in a food processor. Transfer to a pitcher, then stir in rose syrup, lemon juice, and rosewater.

Strain mixture through a sieve into a medium bowl, pressing pulp with a ladle. Transfer strained mixture back to pitcher.

Pour mixture into ice-pop molds (available at most grocery stores), leaving a little room at the tops. Insert sticks and freeze until solid, about 5 hours. Unmold and serve.

A FEW MORE SEASONAL OPTIONS

Blueberry & Mint

5 cups Blueberries + 1/4 cup Fresh Mint

Strawberry

4 cups Strawberries + 1/4 cup Fresh Lemon Balm + 2 tbsp Lemon

Watermelon & Hibiscus

4 cups Cubed Watermelon + 1 tbsp Hibiscus + 1 tsp Ginger + 2 tbsp Lime

HONEYSUCKLE
ELIXIR

INGREDIENTS

2 tbsp honeysuckle
1 1/2 vanilla beans
1/4 tsp cinnamon chips
1 tbsp honey
4 oz vodka or glycerin

EQUIPMENT
2 –2oz or 4 oz bottle with dropper top
4 oz jar with lid
cheesecloth or strainer

PREPARATION

Mix all ingredients in a 4 oz jar. Shake well mixiing all ingredients together. Label with all ingredients and date.

Shake every other day. Infuse for 4-6 weeks. Strain and pour into a dropper botle or jar with lid. Label and date.

How to drink Honeysuckle Nectar

This is how you drink honeysuckle nectar:
- Carefully pinch the bottom of the flower, not all the way through, just enough to cut the petals

- Then gently pull the end, which should pull the style through.

- The style will scrape the nectar from the inside of the petal, and you'll see a tiny drop of nectar, which is all sugar water with a tiny amount of fragrance.

HONEYSUCKLE
MINI POUNDCAKE

Every country kid at some point growing up heard that pleading call of "no running in the house, I have a cake in the oven" or "don't make my cake fall". Both were signals that delicious cake was in the near future. My favorite was always my Mom's pound cake. The smell of that perfect balance of butter and vanilla floating through the air is priceless. To this day when I need a lil sweetness and softness in my life I'll bake some mini poundcakes. A few for me and a few for sharing with friends.

INGREDIENTS
3 cups flour
3 cups sugar
5 eggs
1 1/2 cups butter, softened
1/2 cup milk
1 tbsp honeysuckle elixir
1 tsp baking powder

EQUIPMENT
measuring spoons and cups
medium and large size bowls
electric mixer
wood or silicone spoon
mini cake molds

PREPARATION
Pre-Heat Oven at 350 degrees.

1st Bowl
Mix flour and baking powder thoroughly. Set to the side.

2nd Large Bowl
Pour sugar into bowl mixing softened butter gradually using an electric mixer on low setting. Mix until creamy texture. Next, add eggs gradually one at time into the bowl, mixing consistently.

Alternate adding milk and flour baking powder mixture into the bowl. Stir in Honeysuckle elixir, mix well. Pour batter into mini cake molds half way.

Bake at 350 degrees for 25-28 minutes. Remove from the oven and place the pound cakes, right side up, on a wire rack, and let cool for 10-12 minutes. This allows the cake to become firm enough to remove from the pan without breaking apart.

BLACKBERRY
COMPOTE

I loved picking blackberries along my Grandparents fence line when I was a kid. Dark, juicy and refreshing. When my cousins and I saw my Granddaddy Edward picking them we knew that my Grandma Geraldines' beyond delicious cobbler was not too far behind. Few things bring me joy like a freshly baked warm blackberry cobbler and my Grandma made the best.

INGREDIENTS
2 1/2 cup blackberries
3 tbsp honey
1/8 tsp ginger; grated
1 lemon
1/4 tsp rose water
1 tsp cornstarch
water

EQUIPMENT
measuring spoons and cups
spoon
medium size bowl
medium saucepan

Did You Know:
Blackberries contain high levels of antioxidants to fight against the adverse impact of free radicals in the body. Free radicals can damage cells and are thought to be closely involved in the aging process.

PREPARATION
Toss the berries in a bowl with 2 tablespoons of raw honey. Mix. Cover and refrigerate overnight. The next day, add 1 more tablespoon of raw honey.

Add 1 tsp of cornstarch and 2 tbsp of water in a bowl. Mix well until cornstarch dissolves. Set aside.

Add blackberry honey mix, ginger, rose water and 1 tsp of lemon juice in a saucepan.

Add 1 tablespoon water, cornstarch mixture and bring to a simmer over medium heat.

Simmer until blackberries begin to break apart, about 8-10 minutes. Stir occasionally from time to time.

Early Morning Fog. Sun Soaked Sunrises,
Ham Rolls, Endless Mountain Ranges, Country Back Roads,
Cassette Tapes...

Mighty Clouds of Joy,
Rev. Shirley Caesar
Rev. James Cleveland
Mississippi Mass Choir,
Sweet Honey in the Rock

...Pick-up Trucks and Cadillacs,
Spring Revivals, Easter Suits & Mother's Day Flowers

~

We must continue to protect our breath, joy and inner sanctuary.
Every day. Sustain our daily practice that care
for our bodies, mind, and spirit.

How we show up for ourselves determines
how we show up in our lives.

~

HIBISCUS BALM AND
HYDRATING SPRAY

Hydrating and energy giving hydrosol spray. Perfect for afternoon cook outs, days at the beach or just running errands on a hot day. The natural acids present in hibiscus help to purify your skin by breaking down dead skin cells while helping control acne breakouts. It's naturally occurring oils also help keep your skin moisturised.

INGREDIENTS

3 quarts distilled water
1 1/2 to 2 cups hibiscus flowers
bags of ice

EQUIPMENT

still
glass bowl (receiver)
vegetable steamer
filter paper
funnel
glass jars and/ or glass spray
bottles

PREPARATION

Pour 3 quarts of water in the still. Mix in hibiscus. Let it sit and infuse for 2-3 hours.

Remove the center post from a metal veggie steamer basket and stand the steamer, spread fully opened, in the center of the pot. Place the receiver bowl on the center of the steamer.

Put the lid right side up on the still. Bring to a boil. When water begins to simmer; reduce heat to low medium. Heat should be high enough to maintain the vaporization of the liquids. Turn the lid upside down on the still.

Place bags full of ice on the lid. Inside the still, the vapor will rise to the cooler lid, condense back to liquid, flow down to the low point of the lid, and drip into the receiver. The receiver will collect the hydrosol and volatile oil. Beware of steam whenever lifting the lid of the pot.

Place a wetted filter paper in a funnel. Place the funnel into a jar or glass spray bottle.

When the hydrosol is cool, pour it through the filter paper. The hydrosol will pass through; if any significant volatile oil is present, it will collect in the bottom of the filter paper. You can collect this volatile oil with a dropper bottle pipette.

Cap the jar or spray bottle. Label with content, date, and refrigerate.

USE

Hydrosol waters can be used in lotions, creams, bath preparations or straight on the skin. Hibiscus oil (the active ingredient in this hydrosol water) is known for its skin soothing benefits as well as its skin toning properties. It is often added to healing skin balms for the treatment of eczema. In this easy to use form, you can spray directly on your skin or use as the water portion in your lotions and healing salves.

JASMINE FACE
AND BODY MIST

INGREDIENTS
1/2 cup jasmine flowers
1/4 cup skullcap leaves
3/4 cup witch hazel
2 tbsp aloe vera gel
5 drops jasmine essential oil.,
optional
8 oz distilled water

EQUIPMENT
2 -4 oz or an 8 oz glass bottle
with spray top
8 oz glass jar with lid
glass bowl
strainer
funnel

Did You Know:

Jasmine Hydrates and restores for softer skin. Increase skin's elasticity and helps balance moisture in the skin to naturally reduce dryness. Jasmines natural antibacterial properties help to protect skin and aid skin's immunity.

PREPARATION
Add jasmine and skullcap to an 8 oz mason jar. Fill the jar to the top with warm to room temperature water and close with lid. Steep for 8 hours or overnight.

Strain into another jar or bowl. Add witch hazel, aloe vera and jasmine essential oil to the container. Stir.

Pour into spray bottles using funnel. Label with contents, date, and refrigerate.

USE
Use it as a face and body mist that can be sprayed directly on to the skin. Use in the mornings and at night before adding moisturizer. Refreshing spritz of jasmine during the day. Leaves skin revived and hydrated.

Keeps for 4-5 months stored in the refrigerator.

MA' DEAR'S
FACIAL STEAM

Steam induces perspiration that aids releasing toxins and increases skin circulation while helping your skin to breathe. The heat helps to warm up the skin, soften, open pores and prepare the skin for a face mask, cream or facial oil.

INGREDIENTS

fresh rose petals
fresh pine needles
fresh lilacs
distilled water

EQUIPMENT

large bowl
towel

PREPARATION

Bring water to a steaming simmer and add to the bowl. Add lilacs, roses, and pine needles.

USE

Place your face over the bowl, being careful not to get too close, the steam can get very hot. Drape a clean toel over your head to cover the bowl and hold in the herbal steam.

Lilac Toner

Lilac flowers have astringent and aromatic qualities. Astringents tighten, draw, and dry the tissues of the skin. Lilacs create a beautiful facial toner.

Add 1/2 cup blossoms, 1/4 cup witch hazel and 3/4 cup distilled water into a 8 oz jar with lid. Be sure the blossoms are completely covered by liquid. If not, add more witch hazel. Store out of direct sunlight.

Infuse for 2-3 weeks, gently shaking every other day to mix. Strain the mixture and pour face toner into a glass spray bottle. The spent blossoms can be composted.

To Use Toner: Apply by spritzer on clean face after washing. Storing in refrigerator is optional. Toner can be stored in a cool location since the witch hazel acts as a preservative.

We Are Born with all the tools, we need only begin picking them up. Feel them. Name them. Use them.

A state of exhaustion will not bring forward our freedom. Rest. Hydrate. Pray. Meditate. Breathe. Begin again.

...I am a trained Yoga and Meditation Instructor but I did not begin my practice at a yoga studio or yoga retreat. It began in the arms of my mother to the sounds and movement of her humming and rocking back and forth...whether in church when there is a momentary lull in the program and an Elder begins a contagious humm that permeates through the pews until either the choir picks up the congregations medicine and evolves into musical healing or the preacher steps forward with a word for our spirits.

Our mothers and grandmothers humming have held and carried us through endless hours working in the fields, cleaning floors, pressing sheets that were not our own, soothing away a toddlers scraps and cuts from a tumble or fall, holding space and healing broken hearts in a world that does not always and may never love them back.

There is scientific research and articles written on the power of the humm as self-soothing sounds that affect us on a physical level, reducing stress, inducing calmness, and enhancing sleep as well as lowering heart rate and blood pressure and producing powerful neurochemicals such as oxytocin, the "love" hormone. But we don't need anyone to validate what we know in our hearts and minds by touch, body and spirit.

Better said as
"I am here because of Grandma's hands and prayers."

CLEOPATRA JONES
MILK BATH

Tamara Dobson...my first memory of watching a Black woman on screen in full ownership of her body, mind, beauty and kicking bad dudes butt with style and grace. All while driving her silver and black '73 Corvette Stingray! While she evokes the glory of a rock goddess, she also reminds me that the luxe part of healing and nourishment is my birthright as well.

Nourishing. Calming. Luxurious Healing Bath.

INGREDIENTS

1/2 cup jasmine flowers
1/4 cup oatstraw
1/2 cup powdered goat milk
1/2 cup powdered oats
1/2 cup himalayan pink salt
10 drops jasmine essential oil, optional
 5 drops patchouli essential oil, optional

EQUIPMENT
measuring cups
medium size bowl
2 - 8 oz glass containers with lid
spoon

PREPARATION

Combine Himlayan Pink Salt with essential oils in a bowl. Set to the side.

Combine oats and goats milk thoroughly. Next, stir in the Himalayan Pink Salt mixture. Add jasmine and oatstraw. Mix well.

Pour Milk Bath mix into glass container with lid. Let mixture rest overnight or 24 hours to infuse herbs with milk, oats, and salt.

USE
Run a warm bath. Gently sprinkle 1 to 2 cups into bath water.

JASMINE-ALOE
SHOWER GEL

This gentle, lightweight cleanser is perfect for those breezy Spring nights. Jasmine helps ease tired muscles, scars and stretch marks. It's fragrant scent makes for an intoxicating stress-buster. Mix with aloe vera for a skin-cooling treat. Cool showers. Moisturizer. Restoration.

INGREDIENTS

1 cup distilled water
1 tbsp jasmine flowers
1/2 cup castile soap
1/4 cup fresh aloe vera gel
2 tbsp jojoba oil
10-15 drops jasmine essential oil

EQUIPMENT
measuring cups and spoons
spoon
funnel
8 to 10 oz pump bottle

PREPARATION

Bring the water to a boil and pour it over the jasmine in a glass bowl. Steep for 15 minutes. Strain. Set to the side and let the tea cool to room temperature.

In a large measuring cup, combine the castile soap and aloe vera. Add 1/4 cup of the jasmine tea to the soap aloe mixture and stir this 1:1 ratio of soap. The gel will be gentle on your skin and create beautiful suds.

Add the jojoba oil, then add essential oil. Transfer the mixture to a bottle with a funnel.

USE
Swirl the bottle, disperse 2 to 3 pumps, and work into a lather all over your body. Rinse and finish.

MAGNOLIA BODY
BUTTER

Consistency is medicine. Touch. I loved climbing and sitting under the large magnolia tree in our back yard as a kid. Magnolia trees have always been a source of peace and strength for me. A guarantee shade spot on a hot afternoon and the perfect climbing challenge for a litle kid in cool evenings.

INGREDIENTS

2 oz magnolia infused grapeseed oil
2 oz oatstraw infused grapeseed oil
3/4 cup cocoa butter
1/4 cup coconut oil
2 tbsp shea Butter
1/4 tsp vitamin E
20 drops of magnolia essential oil, optional

EQUIPMENT
double boiler
blender of hand mixer
wide mouth or cream and lotion jars with lids

PREPARATION

In the double boiler on low heat melt cocoa butter, shea butter and coconut oil. Stirring lightly until the mixture has completely melted.

Using a mixer or blender thouroughly stir in the magnolia and oatstraw infused oils, vitamin E and magnolia essential oil.

Pour the body butter into the jar and close with lid. The body butter will continue to thicken and become solid over a couple of days.

USE
Gently rub palms together warming body butter. Liberally apply to dampened skin after a shower or bath.

JASMINE
MASSAGE OIL

I love using jasmine to make massage oil for sore muscles that come from hours in the garden. The scent always puts me at ease and they often bloom as my lilac blooms are winding down. The jasmine flower is usually white, although some species are yellow or cream, and it can bloom all year long. Jasmine can grow in a pot or hanging basket. It can also be planted directly in the ground and trained to climb or grow as bushes or ground cover.

INGREDIENTS
3/4 cup sweet almond oil
1/4 cup jasmine infused jojoba oil
10 drops jasmine essential oil
4-5 drops bergamot essential oil

PREPARATION
Mix almond and jasmine infused jojoba oils.

Stir in jasmine and bergamot essential oils thoroughly. Pour into a jar or bottle. Add label with contents and date.

USE
Gently rub palms together warming massage oil. Liberally apply and massage into skin.

Did You Know:
Massage...releases endorphins, lactic acid, and histamines, and drains lymph nodes. Toxins are moved for easier elimination. Human touch is important too.

SUN SOOTHER
BALM

This salve is a gentle wound healer, great for treating minor cuts and burns. It has anti-septic quality, and it encorages the growth of new tissues. Rich, protective and nourishing, this all-natural sunscreen is easy to make. Massage it over any area that needs extra protection.

INGREDIENTS
4 oz olive oil
3 tbsp calendula
1 tbsp comfrey
1 tbsp lavender
2 tbsp beeswax
1 tbsp shea butter

EQUIPMENT
4 oz glass jar with lid
measuring spoons
small and medium funnels
glass bowl
small saucepan
2 -2 oz or 4 oz tins or wide
mouth glass container

PREPARATION
Sun Herbal Oil Infusion
Place calendula, comfrey, and lavender in a jar. Pour olive oil covering plant material to the top of the jar leaving 1/8 to 1/4" space at the top. Close with lid. Label w/ contents and date. Place in the sun for infusion. Strain 4 weeks later. If you don't have time for a sun infusion then use the double boiler or stove infusion method.

Making a Healing Balm
Over medium heat, bring a saucepan of water to a simmer. Set a double boiler or heatproof bowl over the pot add shea butter and let it melt. Stir in infused herbal oil. Remove from heat.

Add beeswax. Stir and allow to melt over residual heat.

Pour the mixture into 2 oz or 4 oz wide mouthed containers that you can easily dip into. Let it sit on the counter for a few hours to harden.

SUN HERBAL OIL INFUSION
SEASON REVIEW

A review of the Spring and Summer sun infusions to begin mid to end of spring as plants begin to grow and bloom.

PREPARATION

Sun Herbal Oil Infusion
Place herb(s) in a jar. Pour chosen oil over plant material to the top of the jar leaving 1/8 to 1/4" space at the top. Close with lid. Label with contents and date.

Place in the sun for infusion. Strain 4-6 weeks later. If you don't have time for a sun infusion.

SUN INFUSIONS

Magnolia Body Butter
Magnolia flowers in Grapeseed oil
Oatstraw in Grapeseed oil

Jasmine Soothing Massage Oil
Jasmine flowers & leaves in Jojoba oil

Feeling Good Day and Night Conditioner
Lavender in Jojoba Oil

Sheba, Baby Butter Hair Cream
Bergamot in Jojoba Oil

Mo' Better Curls, Coils & Twist Butter Balm
Hibiscus flowers in Jojoba oil

Herbal Hair Oil
Lavender, Nettles & Rosemary in Jojoba oil

Sun Soother Salve
Calendula, Comfrey & Lavender in Olive oil

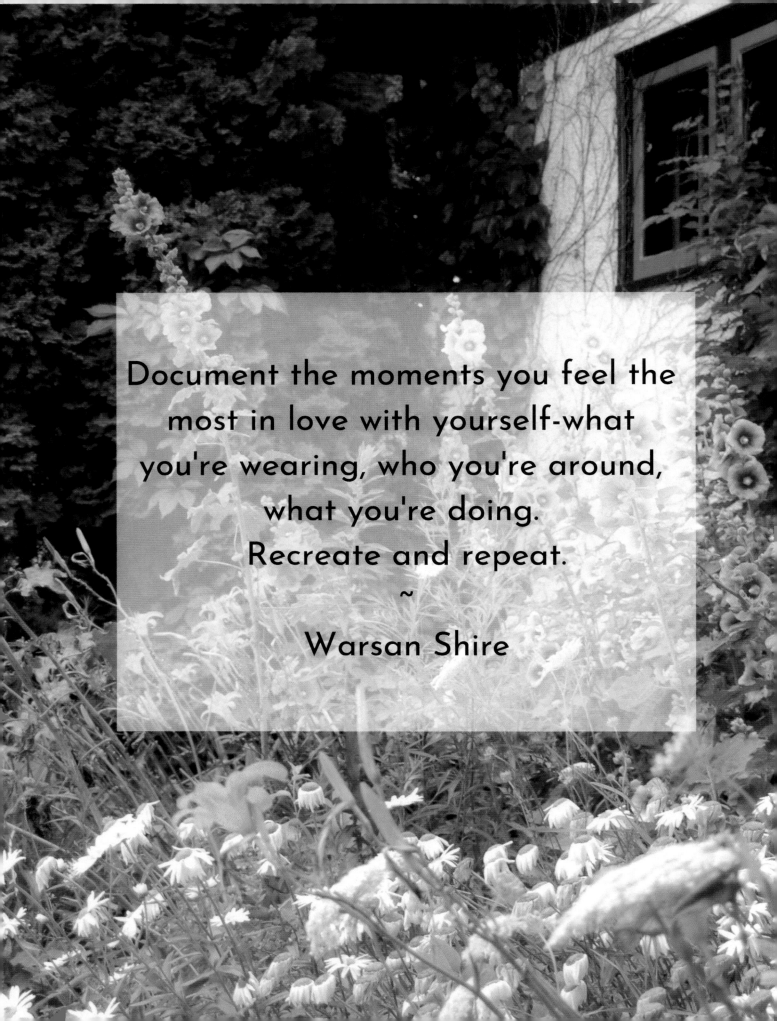

Document the moments you feel the most in love with yourself-what you're wearing, who you're around, what you're doing.
Recreate and repeat.
~

Warsan Shire

SECTION 4

ALIGN

SUMMER

CREATE

RECLAIM THE FUTURE

Summer

...is a time for Picking Cucumbers right off the Vine for the Perfect Salad,
Family Reunions, Weekend Cookouts, Concerts in the Park,
Rambling Front Porch Conversations,
& Late Nights of Ice Cream and Whisky around the Fire Pit.

HERBAL HAIR RINSES
~
SWEETBACK BABY HAIR RINSE
LAKE HIGHLIGHTS
BACKYARD DIAMONDS

SHEBA, BABY BUTTER HAIR CREAM

WATERMELON WATER
~WATERMELON SLUSHIE~

LUCY "SUMMERTIME" SPRITZER

FRONT PORCH SUN TEA

TEACAKE LATTE

COFFEE...THE REAL DEAL
~
HIBISCUS ROSE LATTE
LAVENDER VANILLA LATTE
COFFY ON ICE

FRONT PORCH SUN TEA

ANYTIME IS A GOOD TIME FOR WINE
~
REUNION WINE
HONEYSUCKLE ROSE WHITE WINE
HIBISCUS ROSÉ
BRUNCH IN HARLEM

BLACK RASPBERRY VINEGAR

CUCUMBER SALAD

DANDELION GREENS

PEACH ICE CREAM & WHIPPED
CREAM
~PEACH SLUSHIE~

AFTER HOURS COFFEE RUB

CALENDULA & ALOE FACE
AND BODY MIST

GREEN GARDEN TEA
COOLING SPRAY

WATERMELON & HIBISCUS FACE
AND BODY MIST

MUD PIES & STARLIGHT
CLAY MASK

SOOTHING CALENDULA &
CHAMOMILE CLEANSING GRAINS

SUMMER MOON, HONEY
SUGAR SCRUB CUBES

CUCUMBER MINT SUGAR SCRUB

HERBAL TEA RINSES
SWEET SIMPLE SUPERB

Easy to make and oh so nourishing, herbal hair rinses that can be used right after washing or between washes. They deliver vitamins and minerals to the hair and can bring out subtle tints of color. Because tea rinses don't keep well, I make one treatment at a time and use it immediately. Match your current energy or what is going on in your life.

PREPARATION

Place herbs in a quart jar. Pour hot water over the herbs and fill to the top. Close with lid and steep from 30 minutes to overnight.

Strain the infusion using the cheese cloth. You may need to strain it two or more times to get all the plant mater out. If some sediment remains after you've strained don't worry about it. If you are not using right away then label and refrerate to keep longer.

USE
Cleanse and rinse your hair as you normally do. Then pour the rinse over your head or apply via a spray bottle. Massage into your scalp and work it through to the tips. Leave in or rinse out.

EQUIPMENT
jars with lids
measuring spoons and cups
strainer or cheesecloth
heat resistant bowl

HERBAL TEA RINSES
BEAUTY SURROUNDS

We, ourselves' are high art.
Ntozake Shange

INGREDIENTS

SweetBack Baby Hair Rinse
2 tbsp Chamomile
2 tbsp Rose
5 cups Water

Lake Highlights
4 tbsp Calendula
5 cups Water

Backyard Diamonds
2 tbsp Nettles
1 tbsp Comfry
5 cups Water

SHEBA, BABY
BUTTER HAIR CREAM

I hope you give this recipe a go! I've made hair creams a million different ways and this "no melt" version is the simplest to make yet produces the best , creamiest results. "Sheba, Baby" is in honor of Pam Grier and her ever fly hair. Who doesn't love an over the top movie, bell bottom suits and beautifully coiffed hair.

INGREDIENTS
1/2 cup shea butter
1 tbsp argan oil
1/4 cup coconut oil
3 tbsp bergamot infused jojoba oil

Optional
10 drops bergamot essential oil
5 drops lavender essential oil

EQUIPMENT
large bowl
hand blender
spoon
pipette, optional
wide mouthed jar

PREPARATION
In a large bowl, add the shea and coconut oil. Blend well with a handheld blender and then stir in the jojoba and argan oils. Continue blending for 3-5 minutes. Optional: Stir in essential oils.

Put the butter in a wide mouthed jar. You can also pipe it into your jar if you want a buttercream like look.

USE
To use, scoop out a small dollop of butter and apply using fingertips. Apply to damp or dry hair and scalp. It will absorb quickly and leave you feeling soft and smooth.

WATERMELON
WATER

I'm convinced that the best watermelons are the ones you buy along the road at a fruit stand or from the back of a farmers pick-up truck. Even now it's a summer Saturday routine to get to my neighborhood seller's truck for the best picks of the day. Watermelons are found in many stores but try getting yours from a local seller, farmers market or go to a farm and pick your own.

INGREDIENTS
1 cup watermelon, cubed
12 oz water

EQUIPMENT
cheesecloth or strainer
blender
glass or container

Did You Know:
Watermelon is one of the best food sources of water. Vitamins B1, B6, C, beta carotene, potassium, magnesium, and rich in lycopene. Unlike many fruits, watermelon loses little of its nutritional value when it's cut, so slices can be kept in the referator for a few days.

PREPARATION
Place watermelon in a high speed blender. Turn blender on medium spead and work up to high speed until the watermelon is completely smooth.

Strain though cheesecloth. Enjoy!

*This recipe works great with many different summertime time fruits and vegetables.

Create you own or try one of these:
1/2 cup Strawberries +
1/2 cup Watermelon
1 cup Peach + 1 tsp fresh Ginger
1 cup Blueberries + 2 tbsp Lime

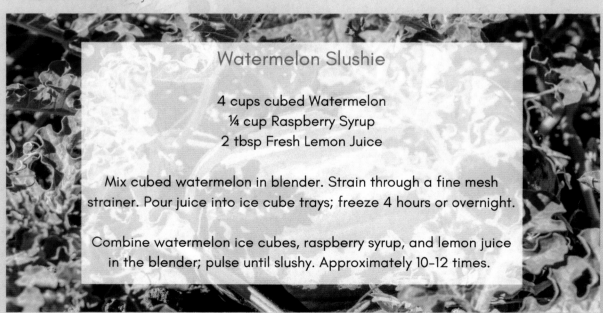

Watermelon Slushie

4 cups cubed Watermelon
¼ cup Raspberry Syrup
2 tbsp Fresh Lemon Juice

Mix cubed watermelon in blender. Strain through a fine mesh strainer. Pour juice into ice cube trays; freeze 4 hours or overnight.

Combine watermelon ice cubes, raspberry syrup, and lemon juice in the blender; pulse until slushy. Approximately 10-12 times.

CUCUMBER
SALAD

Every summer my Uncle Matthew would bring my Grandma Ethel a bunch of cucumbers from his garden and she would make the best cucumber salads I've ever eaten. This easy cucumber salad recipe is the perfect snack on a hot humid afternoon.

INGREDIENTS

1 cup cucumbers
1/4 cup red onion, thinly sliced
1 tbsp fresh thyme
1/2 tsp salt
1/2 tsp pepper
1 1/2 cups organic raw unfiltered apple cider vinegar

EQUIPMENT
bowl
measuring spoons and cups
knife
spoons

PREPARATION

Mix cucumber and onions in a large bowl.

Mix apple cider vinegar, salt, and pepper, in a small bowl. Pour over the cucumbers and onions, and toss to coat.

Sprinkle in fresh chopped thyme and toss the salad. Refrigerate until ready to serve.

Did You Know:
Organic, unfiltered apple cider vinegar also contains a substance called mother, which consists of strands of proteins, enzymes, and friendly bacteria that give the product a murky appearance.

PEACH
ICE CREAM

This delicious homemade ice cream starts by making a custard. This isn't difficult, but you do need to follow a few steps so your custard turns out. I love ice cream and many of my best childhood memories involve something deliciously frozen to cool down on a hot humid day.

INGREDIENTS

2 cups peaches, peeled and chopped
4 egg yolks
3/8 tsp salt
3/4 cup sugar
1 1/2 tsp vanilla extract
2 cups heavy cream
1 cup milk

EQUIPMENT

ice cream maker
electric mixer
medium bowl
wire whisk
medium saucepan
strainer
freezer safe container

PREPARATION

Peaches
Place chopped peached in a bowl. Add 1/4 cup sugar and mix well. Cover and let sit for at least 1 hour.

Once the peaches have released a lot of juice, place peaches and juice in a food processor. Pulse 3-4 times just until peaches are broken up into smaller pieces.

Custard
In a saucepan, heat the heavy cream, milk, salt and 1/2 cup of sugar. Warm over medium heat, stirring often until the sugar has dissolved, 3 -4 minutes.

In a separate bowl, beat the egg yolks with a wire whisk or an electric mixer. Egg yolks will become smooth and lighter in color.

Take 1/2 cup of heated cream mixture and pour slowly into egg yolks. Whisk steadily while pouring in mixture.

Pour egg mixture back into the remaining cream mixture. Reheat over medium heat for 5-8 minutes, stir often. You do not want this mixture to boil. Mixture will begin to slightly thicken. You want it to be thick enough to coat the back of a spoon. An instant read thermometer should be between 175-185 F.

Place a fine strainer over the top of a bowl. Pour the custard mixture into the strainer. Strain off any small bits of egg or lumps. Cover and refrigerate.

ICE CREAM
Make certain your custard is fully chilled (at least 4 hours) before churning.

Your churning bowl should be completley frozen before churning (at least 12 hours). Add custard mixture to your churning bowl and mix according to the directions of your ice cream maker.

Harden ice cream in freezer after churning for at least 2 hours. If ice cream becomes too hard, just let it set at room temperature for 10 minutes before scooping.

Peach Wine Slushies

Ingredients
2 cups cold fruity white wine (I used Sauvignon Blanc)
2-3 medium peaches, blanched, peeled, frozen, and sliced
1 tbsp fresh grated ginger, optional
Sliced peaches for serving, optional topping

Preparation
Combine the wine and peaches (ginger optional) in a blender. Puree until smooth.

If the mixture is too warm and or too liquid like then place it in the freezer and stir every 30 minutes until a perfect slushy texture forms.

You can make these in advance and defrost for 15 minutes at room temperature before serving. You can also double the recipe and use the entire bottle of wine to serve 4.

TEACAKE
LATTE

There's two things everybody got to find out for themselves: they got to find out about love, and they got to find out about living. Now, love is like the sea. It's a moving thing. And it's different on every shore. And living... well... There are years that ask questions and years that answer.

***Their Eyes Were Watching God,* Zora Neale Hurston**

INGREDIENTS
1 cup oat milk
1 tbsp hibiscus flowers
1 tbsp rose petals
1 tsp ginger root
1/4 tsp cinnamon
raw honey
2 cups water

EQUIPMENT
tea kettle
strainer
frother
saucepan

PREPARATION
You can either use a frother to make this latte, or you can make it by heating the milk in a pot. I prefer this with a frother, which gives it that beautiful creamy foam on top.

Frother Method
Steep the hibiscus, rose and ginger root in a pot of hot water for 15-20 minutes. Then pour into a cup. Leaving room at the top for your frothed milk.

Froth the milk in your frother and then fill the cup the rest of the way with the frothed milk.

Stove Top Frothing Method
Pour milk into a sauce pan on low/medium heat. Use a whisk and continue to manually froth the milk a bit. Pour into your cup and enjoy!

COFFEE...
THE REAL DEAL

Delicious option for when you don't want to give up your morning coffee. From Grandma's kitchen to coffee around the world.

INGREDIENTS

Hibiscus Rose Latte
1 cup water
1/2 cup honey
1/4 cup rose petals
1 tsp hibiscus flowers
1 cup coffee, brewed
1/2 cup oat milk, frothed

Lavender Vanilla Latte
1 cup water
1/2 cup honey
3 tbsp lavender
Seeds of 1 vanilla Bean
1 cup coffee, brewed
1/2 cup oat milk, frothed

EQUIPMENT
saucepan
measuring spoons and cups
strainer
frother

PREPARATION

In a saucepan, combine water, honey, herbs and spices. Stir. Bring to a slight boil, then turn to low and let gently simmer for 2-3 minutes. Remove from heat and steep for 20 minutes.

Strain into a lidded container and allow syrup to cool completely.

To make the latte, combine your coffee and 1-2 tbsp of syrup in a mug.

Froth the oat milk in your frother and then fill the cup the rest of the way with the frothed milk.

Store any unused syrup in the refrigerator.

Coffy On Ice

Today was a Good Day Cubes
Stir your honey, favorite extracts (like honeysuckle, vanilla, hazelnut) or spices (ginger or cinnamon) into milk of your choice. Freeze in ice cube trays, then use the cubes to chill your coffee, which will get flavored as they melt.

Blended Chill
Create a smoothie using your brewed coffees as a base. Blend coffee, cashew butter, plain yogurt, banana, oats/oat flour and cinnamon. The oats are great thickeners but also add fiber.

AFTER HOURS
COFFEE RUB

This homemade coffee rub is the ultimate rub when you want to bring a savory and slightly spicy flavor to your meat. Great for BBQ and grilling. This homemade coffee rub is the ultimate rub when you want to bring a savory and slightly spicy flavor to your meat. The ingredient that ties this rub all together is the earthy flavor of the coffee, making it a perfect rub for beef.

INGREDIENTS
2 1/2 tbsp instant coffee
2 tbsp smoked paprika
2 tbsp sea salt
2 tbsp garlic powder
1 tbsp onion powder
1 tbsp black pepper
1 tsp chili powder
3/4 tsp cayenne

PREPARATION
Mix all ingredients in a bowl. Use a fork to crush any clumps of seasonings. Store in an airtight container for up to a month.

We call our food soul food. We are the only people who named our cuisine after something invisible that you can feel like love and God. Something completely transcendental. It's about a connection between our dead and those waiting to be born.

Michael Twitty, Culinary Historian

MUD PIES & STARLIGHT
CLAY MASK

Summers as a kid in my rural community seemed normal to me growing up but now many decades later I realize how much of a magical gift it really was. My cousins and I would start each day with nothing but our imaginations as our guide to seek out the next adventure. Hot humid afternoons spent running under the water hose, making rainbows, mud pies bake-offs, and evenings filled with chasing lightning bugs in the yard.

INGREDIENTS
1 1/2 tsp jasmine or rose hydrosol
1 tbsp Moroccan red clay powder
1 tsp oatstraw infused grapeseed oil

EQUIPMENT
non-metal bowl
spoon
make-up brush
washcloth, optional

Did You Know:
Moroccan clay has mineral rich properties that gently draw out toxins and dirt while refining and softening skin texture, tightening pores, removing blackheads, purifies and detoxifies the skin.

PREPARATION
In a non-metal bowl mix Moroccan Red Clay Powder with Grapeseed oil. Mix until smooth. Gradually mix in hydrosol.

To Use
Apply evenly on damp face and neck using your fingers or a clean make-up brush. Leave on for 10-15 minutes; remove with warm water in circular motions with your fingers or a washcloth.

* For sensitive skin please patch test before using the mask

SUMMER MOON, HONEY
SUGAR SCRUB CUBES

I've been making and using sugar scrubs for most of my life. There is just something scrumptious in feeling sugar glide across your skin after a long day. One of the reasons for the smooth and less abrasive feeling is due to sugar granules being rounder than salt. This makes sugar a gentler exfoliant for breaking down layers of dead skin to give us smooth skin. It also speeds up rehydration, keeping skin conditioned and moisturized. Give them a try or try creating your own recipe.

> I want to live the rest of my life, however long or short, with as much sweetness as I can decently manage, love all the people I love, and doing as much as I can of the work I still have to do. I am going to write fire until it comes out of my ears, my eyes, my nose holes--everywhere, until it's every breath I breathe.
>
> ~
> Audre Lorde

PREPARATION

Grate the melt & pour soap base with a cheese grater or chop it if you prefer. Place the soap base in a small saucepan on low heat, and watch closely. Once melted, add the shea butter and coconut oil. Whisk well.

Once melted, remove from the heat and allow to cool slightly to prevent the sugar from melting. After the mixture has cooled, add the sugar and optional color agent. Stir quickly and thoroughly. Add the essential oils, and mix again.

Scoop the sugar scrub into the silicone molds. Optional, place dried herbs like rose petals on the top cubes while they are still wet. Place the silicone molds in the freezer for 30 minutes to set. Carefully remove the sugar cubes, and store them in an airtight glass container.

Notes:
Natural color options include: beet powder, rose petal powder, and hibiscus powder. You purchase or grind your own into a fine powder.

If you don't have a silicone mold on a hand, you can also try using small muffin tins or ice cube trays.

SUMMER MOON, HONEY
SUGAR SCRUB CUBES

These homemade sugar scrub cubes gently cleanse, exfoliate, and moisturize, leaving dry skin feeling softer and more hydrated They're crafted with natural ingredients, such as coconut oil, shea butter, and melt and pour soap. Plus. they're lightly fragranced with essential oils for soothing and relaxing scents. Treat yourself to these body polishing sugar scrub are an aromatic treat for your skin and your senses.

EQUIPMENT

- cheese grater
- knife (optional)
- small Sauce pan
- whisk
- silicone molds
- airtight glass containers

PREPARATION

Southern Charm
3/4 cup melt & pour soap base, grated
1/2 shea butter
3 tbsp coconut oil
1 cup fine cane sugar
15-20 drops magnolia essential oil

Mountain Views & Pick-up Trucks
3/4 cup melt & pour soap base, grated
1/2 cup shea butter
1 cup fine cane sugar
15 drops cedar essential oil

Summer Lovin'
3/4 cup melt & pour soap base, grated
1/2 cup cocoa butter
3 tbsp coconut oil
1 cup fine cane sugar
15 drops rose essential oil
8-10 drops neroli essential oil
1 tbsp rose petals
1 tbsp natural color, optional

Sleep Like You Mean It
3/4 cup melt & pour soap base, grated
1/2 cup shea butter
3 tbsp coconut oil
1 cup fine cane sugar
15-20 drops lavender
5-6 drops frankincense essential oil
1 tbsp natural color, optional

SOOTHING CALENDULA & CHAMOMILE
CLEANSING GRAINS

Cleansing grains are a powdered face cleanser and gentle exfoliator. The grains are typically made from a few simple ingredients such as: herbs, oats, and clay. The ingredients of choice are blended together to cleanse, exfoliate, and transform your skin. You combine a small amount of the powdered blend with a few drops of water in the palm of your hand, and cleanse your face and body.

INGRDIENTS

1/2 cup of oats
3 tbsp chamomile flowers
3 tbsp calendula flowers
1 tbsp oatstraw
1/2 cup bentonite clay
1 tbsp activated charcoal
water or milk

EQUIPMENT

non-metal measuring cups and spoons
coffee grinder
fine mesh strainer
non-metal bowl
pipette
non-metal spoon
8 oz glass jar with lid

PREPARATION

Add oats, oatstraw, chamomile and calendula to coffee grind. Grind them into fine individual powders.

Combine the powders, pour powdered herbal mix through a fine mesh strainer into a non-metal bowl.

> Note: Metal tools can interfere with clay so go with plastic, wood, or ceramic.

Portion out and add the clay with a non-metal measuring spoon. Transfer to a glass jar with an airtight lid.

To Use

Pour 1-2 teaspoons into the palm of your hand and mix in a tiny amount of tap water, making a paste.

> Note: You can get the skin-softening benefits of lactic acid by using milk instead of water or hibiscus water or green tea for a dose of age fighting antioxidants.

Use your fingertips to massage the paste into your skin, working in circular motions. Rinse with water. Gentle, use daily.

Store in a lidded jar and use within 1 year.

LUCY "SUMMERTIME"
SPRITZER

The perfect fruity and spunky summertime drink created for my niece, Lucy, named after our Great Grandma Lucy. She has the same tilt to her mouth and and in one easy smile says she's "unbothered and living her best life".

INGREDIENTS

1 cup blackberries
1 cup blueberries
1 cup strawberries
1/4 cup raspberries
mint simple syrup
handful of mint leaves
24 oz soda water
Ice, optional

EQUIPMENT

4 – glasses or pitcher
stirrer

PREPARATION

Glasses
Pour fresh or frozen fruit evenly into 4 glasses.

Add 2-3 ice cubes, and pour soda water and 2 tbsp mint simple syrup into each glass.

Stir each glass using a stirrer or knife to mix the fruit throughout the drink.

Garnish with mint sprigs. Serve while cold.

Pitcher
Pour soda water and mint simple syrup (to taste) into the pitcher. Stir.

Add ice cubes (optional) and fruit. Stir. Garnish with mint sprigs. Serve while cold.

FRONT PORCH
SUN TEA

INGREDIENTS
2 1/2 tbsp peppermint
2 1/2 tbsp lemon balm
1 tbsp tulsi
1 lemon
raw unfiltered honey, to taste
water
ice, optional

EQUIPMENT
tea bags
small bowl
64 oz glass pitcher or container
measuring spoons and cups
pot
strainer
spoon or stirrer

PREPARATION

Make the tea:
Add herbs to bowl; mix. Evenly distribute the herb mix into tea bags.

Place tea bags into a glass container. Fill with water and close with lid.

Sun Infusion:
Place outside where the sunlight can strike the pitcher for about 3 to 5 hours. If necessary move the pitcher to keep it in the sun. Remove from the sun when the tea has reached its desired taste and strength. Remove the tea bags and add if honey if desired. Refrigerate.

Tea Time:
The tea will might taste a bit milder than what you are used to from using boiling water. The slow steeping has a way of bringing out a slightly more subtle flavor the plants.

ANYTIME IS A GOOD TIME FOR HERBAL WINE

Making infused wine with fruit and herbs is one of my favorite things to do especially during the summer! It's super simple, adds a deliciously subtle flavor and is a great way to bring new life to wine. I've had a very fruitful few years of mint, raspberries and blackberries growing along my fence line and decided to add a fruity infused wine.

PREPARATION

For every pint of wine, use approximately 1-2 oz dried herbs and or spices.

Add herbs and spices in a jar and pour the wine over. Cap this tightly and shake well. Store the infusing jars in a cool place, out of direct light.

Keep in an easily accessible location so you can shake the jar every other day during the 1-2 week infusion process.

Depending on the wine and the combination of herbs and spices, it may only take a week or so for a delicious, subtly-flavored beverage. If you leave the infusions too long, they may be just too strong. After that, strain the herbs using a strainer and cheesecloth, and return to a jar or a bottle.

You can add some sugar or honey to taste.

The wines should store for a few months if they are well-capped.

The process for creating wines infused with herbs can be adjusted depending on your needs and inspiration. You can choose store bought or homemade wine, and both red and white wines make for delicious concoctions.

HERBAL WINE CONTINUED

INGREDIENTS

Reunion Wine
750ml/1.5 pints White wine (try sauvignon blanc)
1 cup Blackberries, slightly muddled
Fresh Peppermint (approx. 15-20 leaves)

Honeysuckle Rose White Wine
750ml/1.5 pints White wine (try Chardonnay)
3 tbsp Rose Petals
1 tbsp Honeysuckle
1 tsp Vitex

Hibiscus Rosé
750ml/1.5 pints Rosé wine
2 tbsp Hibiscus Flowers
2 tbsp Sumac
2 tsp Ginger dried root

Brunch in Harlem
750ml/1.5 pints Dry white wine (try Pinot Grigio)
2 tbsp Rose Petals
1 tbsp Lavender
2 tsp Skullcap
1 tsp Clove

I like to do the infusions in mason jars and then when I strain, I decant them into pretty bottles. Note: Use clean and sterilized jars and bottles to maintain flavor and integrity.

BLACK RASPBERRY
VINEGAR

INGREDIENTS
1 cup black raspberries
2 cups apple cider vinegar

EQUIPMENT
measuring spoons and cups
8 oz jar with lid
pint jar with lid
strainer
cheesecloth
fork

Did You Know:

Red and black raspberries are rich in nutrients like fiber and vitamin C and are similar in size, flavor, and structure. However, black raspberries are higher in antioxidants than red raspberries.

PREPARATION
Fill a clean jar with whole black raspberries, pressing down slightly to fit in jar snugly. Add enough vinegar to cover raspberries. Cover mixture and let infuse at room temperature for 1 week.

Can't wait a week?

Warm the vinegar over low heat. The warming is important for the vinegar to draw out the black raspberries a lot faster.

Add the black raspberries to the warm (to the touch) vinegar.

Using a fork mash the black raspberries in the bowl. Stir and mix well. Continue with below steps.

Set a strainer over a medium bowl; line with a double layer of cheesecloth. Pour vinegar mixture through strainer. Gather corners of cheesecloth and twist to release juices just until thicker juices begin to strain from cheesecloth. Discard cheesecloth with solids. Pour vinegar into a clean 8-ounce bottle or jar. Cover; chill up to 6 months.

DANDELION GREENS SALAD

This is one my favorite salads and it is so healthy for you! From the root to flowers, dandelion are very nutritious plants. Dandelions are full of vitamins, minerals and fiber. Dandelion greens can be eaten cooked or raw and serve as a great source for vitamins A, C and K. They also contain vitamin E, folate and small amounts of other B vitamins.

INGREDIENTS

2 cups dandelion greens
1/4 cup red onion, chopped
1 tomato, chopped
salt and pepper to taste, optional

Dressing
1 tbsp olive oil
1 tbsp black raspberry vinegar

EQUIPMENT
measuring spoons and cups
medium bowl

PREPARATION

In a small bowl, whisk olive oil and black raspberry vinegar.

In a large bowl, combine dandelion greens, red onion, tomatoes, salt, and pepper.

Drizzle with dressing; toss to coat.

Did You Know:
Dandelions have tap roots that gather nutrients deep down in the soil and bring them up towards the surface, which helps the other surrounding plants. They also help to aerate the soil.

CALENDULA & ALOE REFRESHING
FACE & BODY WIPES

INGREDIENTS

1 cup witch hazel
1/4 cup calendula
1/4 cup rose
3 tbsp aloe vera gel
1 1/2 tbsp glycerin, optional
30 cotton pads

EQUIPMENT
measuring spoons and cups
8 oz wide mouth glass container
with lid
fine mesh strainer
medium bowl
spoon
funnel

PREPARATION

Calendula and roses are perfect plants to infuse with witch hazel for light and soothing smell. Calendula and rose petals are packed with antioxidants that can calm skin irritation and help reverse signs of aging.

Place herbs in a jar and pour the witch hazel over them, then close with lid and shake to coat the petals. The witch hazel will turn a beautiful pinkish color.

Store the infusion in a cool, dry place and let it sit for 1 to 2 weeks. Shake the jar every other day or so.

Using a fine-mesh strainer, pour the liquid into a medium bowl, filtering out and discarding the calendula and roses.

Add the aloe vera and stir together with a spoon until mixed well. Stack your face pads in the second jar, pressing them together tightly.

Slowly pour the witch hazel aloe vera mixture over the pads until fully saturated. Save any leftover liquid for your next batch.

Replace the lid, and flip the jar over to fully disperse the liquid. Allow 1 hour for the pads to soak up all that juice.

To Use
Pick up a pad with clean, dry fingers. Wipe over your face or other areas in need of a clean sweep. Gentle. Use daily. Use within 3 months.

Want to use a mist instead? Mix ¼ cup infused witch hazel with 1 1/2 tbsp of aloe vera and 1 1/2 tbsp of glycerin. Pour into a spray bottle using a funnel. Use the spray as a refreshing mist or after cleansing to hydrate and tone. Avoid your eye area.

GREEN TEA
COOLING SPRAY

INGREDIENTS

1 tbsp nettles
1 tsp skullcap
1/4 cucumber/2 tbsp cucumber juice
1 tbsp aloe vera gel
10 drops peppermint essential oil
1 cup water

EQUIPMENT

small saucepan
hand blender
measuring spoons and cups
pipette
2 -4 oz or 1 -8 oz glass bottle
with fine mist sprayer

PREPARATION

Add nettles and skullcap to container. Pour 1 cup of hot water over herbs. Steep for 20-25 minutes. Strain. Compost plant material. Refrigerate tea.

Peel and puree 1/2 cucumber, then strain and discard the solids. Add 2 tbsp cucumber juice and aloe vera gel to a small spray bottle. Shake and mix well.

Optional: Add peppermint essential oil drops.

Fill the rest of the bottle with the herbal tea and shake well to combine.

To Use

Use as desired. Store in the fridge for 7 to 10 days

WATERMELON & HIBISCUS
FACE AND BODY MIST

INGREDIENTS

1 cup watermelon juice
1/4 cup hibiscus hydrosol
3/4 cup witch hazel
1 tbsp aloe vera juice
1 tsp hibiscus flowers

EQUIPMENT

measuring spoons and cups
glass cup
2 -4 oz or 1 -8 oz glass bottle
with fine mist sprayer
small funnel
empty tea bags or cheese cloth

PREPARATION

Place watermelon in a high-speed blender. Turn blender on medium speed and work up to high speed, until watermelon is completely smooth. Strain through cheesecloth.

Add the witch hazel and hibiscus hydrosol to the glass cup. Fill the empty tea bag with hibiscus flowers. Place tea bag 1/2 way into the liquid. Allow to sit/steep in the liquid for a minute or until you achieve the pink color you like.

Combine all ingredients in large spouted measuring cup and stir well with spoon. Transfer liquid into glass spray bottle(s) using the small funnel. Attach sprayer.

To Use

Use morning and night on skin before moisturizer or during the day for a refreshing pick me up. Store in fridge for up to 3 months.

CUCUMBER MINT SUGAR BODY POLISH

Sugar body polishes brighten tired, dull-looking skin to promote healthy, smooth, and flawless skin. A benefit of a sugar polishes is that they can be used all over our body, not just the face. Just like the face, our body needs exfoliation, too! Add the light cool energy of cucumber and you have a polish perfect for awakening the skin with a smooth finish.

INGREDIENTS

1/4 cucumber; unpeeled
7-10 fresh peppermint leaves
3/4 cup white sugar
2 tsp coconut oil; softened
8-10 drops peppermint essential oil, optional

EQUIPMENT

bowl
spoon
8 oz wide mouth glass container with lid
measuring spoons and cup
hand blender

PREPARATION

Use hand blender to puree the cucumber until all the skin is in tiny flecks.

Next, add the coconut oil and sugar. Blend until the oil is absorbed. Stir in the mint leaves. Store in an airtight container.

Store the sugar scrub in the refrigerator to due to the fresh cucumber.

USE

You can just scoop out what I'll need into a small bowl right before using.

SUN HERBAL OIL INFUSION
SEASON REVIEW FOR FALL

A review of the sun infusions to begin mid to end of spring as plants begin to grow and bloom.

PREPARATION
Sun Herbal Oil Infusion
Place herb(s) in a jar. Pour chosen oil over plant material to the top of the jar leaving 1/8 to 1/4" space at the top. Close with lid. Label with contents and date.

Place in the sun for infusion. Strain 4-6 weeks later.

SUN INFUSIONS

Peace & Quiet Sleep Balm
2 part Lavender, 1 part Rose, & 1 part Skullcap infused in 4 oz grapeseed oil

Stress & Anxiety Release
1 part Peppermint and 1 part Eucalyptus infused in 4 oz olive oil

DAP Hand & Foot Salve
Magnolia infused in 4 oz olive oil
Oatstraw infused in 4 oz olive oil

Pop's Don't Take No Stuff Multi-Purpose, Salve
Black Walnut infused in 4 oz olive oil
2 part Chamomile, 1 part Calendula & 1 part Nettle infused 4 oz olive oil

SECTION 5

ALIGN

FALL

CREATE

RECLAIM THE FUTURE

Allow softness to enter and rest here. Elevate yourself from simple survival mode into a full celebration of life.

FALL

We will be ready or we will be tired when the future arrives. Rest. Dance. Laugh. Eat well. Sleep well. Breathe deeply. Rest.

HERBAL LUXE LOCS BUILD-UP REMOVER

APPLE CIDER VINEGAR SCALP SCRUB

RICH COCONUT & SWEET POTATO HAIR MASK

ME, YOU, & YO COUSINS HAIR CREAM

GRANDDADY'S SMOKEHOUSE CHAI

MAMA LILY'S HERBAL AUTUMN TONIC

UNCLE JR'S SHELTER FROM THE STORM

BACKYARD, MONEY HONEY

WILD DANDELION ROOT TINCTURE

BLACK WALNUT EXTRACT

MR. GILMORE'S WALNUT BUTTER

LAVENDER & WALNUT FUDGE

WALNUT & FLAX BARS

NIGHTS LIKE THIS...REVIVAL NIGHT CANDY

SWEET POTATO ICE CREAM & OH SO FRESH WHIPPED CREAM

SWEET POTATO BUTTER

APPLE CIDER MOLASSES

SWEET POTATO & NUTMEG FACE MASK

APPLE CIDER VINEGAR & ROSE TONER

ETHEL MAE'S NIGHTTIME FACE SERUM

SOOTHING HERBAL BUBBLE BATH

EXFOLIATING & MOISTURIZING BODY WRAP

REVITALIZING HERBAL DETOX BODY WRAP

EXFOLIATING & MOISTURIZING BARS

CHAI 'NILLA BODY OIL

HERBAL LUXE LOCS
BUILD-UP REMOVER

INGREDIENTS

1 1/2 cups distilled water
1 1/2 tbsp apple cider vinegar
2 tbsp lavender
1 tbsp nettles

EQUIPMENT

measuring spoons and cups
small saucepan
french press or medium glass
bowl
fine mesh strainer
2 –6 oz spray bottles
funnel

PREPARATION

Bring the water to a boil in the small saucepan or kettle. Remove from heat.

Add lavender and nettles to a fresh press or glass bowl. Pour hot water over the herbs. Steep for 30 minutes.

Remove the herb with a mesh strainer. Compost the herbs.

Pour the liquid into a spray bottle with a funnel. Add the apple-cider vinegar and shake.

USE

To use, spray or pour the rinse all over your hair after shampooing. Massage into your scalp and comb(finger) through the ends of your hair.

Let the mixture sit for a few minutes and then wash it out with the warm water. For a more potent effect, you can forgo the final rinse. Don't worry you won't end up smelling like vinegar

APPLE CIDER VINEGAR
SCALP SCRUB

INGREDIENTS
1 cup distilled water
2 tbsp cup raw apple cider vinegar
1/4 cup aloe vera gel
1/2 cup Moroccan red clay/ rhassoul clay
2 tsp rosemary
1 tsp nettles
1 tsp almond oil

EQUIPMENT
non-metal mixing spoons
non-metal medium bowl
measuring spoons and cup
6 oz wide mouth glass container with lid

Did You Know:
Apple cider vinegar clarifies and exfoliates your scalp, removing dead skin as well as product buildup that blocks the pores on your scalp.

PREPARATION
Steep nettles and rosemary in 1 cup of hot water for 25-30 minutes. Strain and set aside to cool in a mixing bowl.

Once tea is cooled, add apple cider vinegar, aloe vera gel, almond oil and clay. Stir until blended well.

Pour into a glass container with a lid. Store in the refrigerator for up to 4 weeks.

USE
Massage onto scalp in sections, rinse thoroughly and follow up with the apple cider vinegar hair rinse.

RICH COCONUT SWEET
POTATO HAIR MASK

A great way to strengthen your strands is with more protein, so try this delicious mask. It also gives you a moisturizing boost with the restorative power of coconut milk and it's healing sweetness in slowing hair loss.

INGREDIENTS

1/2 cup of a sweet potato
1 tbsp coconut milk
1 tbsp argan oil
1 tsp oat powder
1 tsp olive oil
1 tsp honey

EQUIPMENT
measuring spoons and cups
small saucepan
fork or potato masher
whisk or spoon
towel
bowl
blender, optional

PREPARATION

Boil sweet potatoes with the skin on for 20-30 minutes. Strain.

Cut a few cuts in the skin from end to end and rub the skin off. Place in bowl and use a potato masher or folk to mash. You can also use a blender to puree the sweet potatoes.

Stir in the coconut milk and oat powder, mix well.

Stir in honey, argan oil and olive oil. Mix well. Let cool until lukewarm.

USE
Apply to damp or dry hair; apply the mask generously so that each tendril is saturated. Drape a towel around your shoulders to avoid drips or apply in the shower. Cover with a satin scarf or shower cap

Wear the mask for 10 to 15 minutes. Do not let it dry or it will be hard to remove.
Rinse your hair thoroughly. Follow up with a co-wash and conditioner.

ME, YOU, & YO COUSINS
HAIR CREAM

INGREDIENTS

1/4 cup shea butter
1/4 cup unrefined organic virgin coconut oil
1 tbsp sweet almond oil
1 tbsp jojoba oil
5 drops vitamin E
15-20 drops neroli essential oil or your choice, optional

EQUIPMENT

large mixing bowl
silicone or wooden mixing spatula
4oz wide-mouth jar with lid
hand mixer with whisk attachment

PREPARATION

Add shea butter to bowl and mix for 2-3 minutes to break up the larger lumps.

If the butter is really cold and hard because some people refrigerate their butter, take it out for a couple hours to a whole day ahead of time.

Mix in ¼ cup coconut oil for a 2-3 minutes.

If your coconut oil is cold and in a solid - state do not microwave it or heat up over the stove. Just sit it out a couple hours ahead of time or add it to the mix as a solid and it will warm up as it's being mixed.

Next add sweet almond oil, jojoba oil, vitamin E oil. Mix for 3-5 minutes or until you start to see peaks forming in the butter.

Use your spatula to scrape the sides of the bowl. Stir and make sure there are no lumps larger than a bean size. Break up any lumps by mixing for another 3-4 minutes if needed. Next use your whisk to break up any small lumps left and to create a smooth butter like cream. Whisk for 4-5 minutes if needed.

Optional: Stir in essential oil of choice.

Add your butter to container by spoon, spatula or pipping into container with lid. You may need to tap the sides of the container to help cream settle and avoid air bubbles.

Shelf Life: 3-4 months.

Granddaddy...chop wood, carry water...long days in the fields and evenings in his smoke house...the scent of tobacco, Virginia ham, leather, tools of every kind, a single light.

Now as an adult, I understand. There is nothing like having a space where you can go, have a sip of tea, tinker around on a project and get your mind right.

GRANDDADDY'S
SMOKEHOUSE CHAI

INGREDIENTS

1 1/2 tsp rooibos
1 tsp roses
1/2 tsp tulsi
4-5 whole cloves
2 star anise
1/2 tsp ginger root
1/4 tsp cinnamon chips
2 cardamom pods
1/8 tsp whole black pepper
honey to taste, optional
oat milk, optional
water

EQUIPMENT

kettle
small saucepan
measuring spoons

PREPARATION

Bring 2 cups of water to a boil in a medium pot. Add cloves, star anise, ginger, cinnamon, cardamom pods, and black pepper. Reduce heat to a low simmer decoction for 30 minutes.

Steep the rooibos, rose, tulsi tea in 1 cup of hot water. Steep for 25-30 minutes.

Strain. Compost plant matter.

Mix tea infusion with the spice decoction at a 1 to 1 ratio. Add milk and honey to taste, optional.

Optional

Leave space to top off your cup with frothed oat milk. Froth the oat milk in your frother and then fill the cup the rest of the way with the frothed milk.

MAMA LILY'S
SEASONAL TONIC

INGREDIENTS
1 tbsp sassafras root
1/2 tsp ginger root
1 lemon
honey
2 cups of water

EQUIPMENT
measuring spoons
saucepan

PREPARATION
Bring 2 cups of water to a boil. Reduce to a simmer. Add sassafras and ginger root. Decoct at a low simmer for 30-35 minutes. Strain.

Optional:
Add lemon juice and honey, to taste.

USE
Drink 1-2 times a day for 5 days when changing seasons.

Yield: 1 cup

*Sassafras is a great health tonic, alterative, diuretic, and stimulant. We use this especially as the seasons change from Fall and in preparation of Winter.

It is recommend that you consult with a healthcare practitioner before using herbal products, particularly if you are pregnant, nursing, or on any medications.

*...and call them greens and
grow on them,
we hum them and make music.
call it our wildness then,
we are lost from the field
of flowers, we become
a field of flowers.
call it our craziness
our wildness
call it our roots,
it is the light in us...*

Roots, Lucille Clifton

Uncle Jr's Homegoing was my first experience in the practice of releasing grief...I will never forget leaving the church and heading to where my uncle's body would be laid to rest. As we were driving along the road I was peering out the window watching the trees go by when I looked slightly down and noticed that the cars going in the opposite direction were all pulling to the side, stopping and getting out of their vehicles in respect for my Uncle, Jr.

Everyone in town and the surrounding towns knew it was his funeral procession and in that moment I knew that what mattered in life was not titles, possessions, power or money but how you conduct yourself and treat everyone you meet in your day to day life.

I have never seen another procession experience like that since. Like most Elders in my family my Uncle Jr. "didn't take no stuff' but if he counted you as family or friend there was nothing that he wouldn't move in space and time to keep you safe, cared for and well fed. Like I said, he was a big man...he loved to eat. But, trust if he ate, you ate. Whatever he had, he would share. I will remember and pass on his kind spirit, his love of dancing, and his deep contagious laughter with me as I move through this life journey.

Through our own healing journeys it is for us to tap into and accept love from others.

UNCLE JR'S
SHELTER FROM THE STORM

INGREDIENTS
1 tbsp astragalus root
1 1/2 tsp burdock root
1 tsp chicory root
1 tsp ginger root
1 tsp virgin coconut oil
3 cups water

2 tsp shatavari root
1/2 tsp hawthorn berry
1 cup oat milk
honey, to taste

EQUIPMENT
measuring spoons
small saucepan
medium saucepan
frother

PREPARATION
Decoct astragalus, burdock, chicory and ginger in 3 cups of water for 30-40 minutes. Strain.

Decoct shatavari and hawthorn berries in oat milk for 30 minutes. Strain.

Pour 1st herbal decoction in to mug or container leaving room for frothed milk.

Optional: coconut oil and honey, to taste.

Froth the shatavari hawthorn infused milk in your frother. Next fill cup with the frothed milk.

**How much we must have looked like stars to stars.
Alysia Nicole Harris**

BACKYARD
MONEY, HONEY

Infusing honey with herbs is a wonderful way to extract the healing properties of a plant and bring those benefits to your skin. Honey draws out water-soluble vitamins like vitamin C, astringent tannins and the natural acids and aromatics from the herbs. The infused honey will be fragrant and flavorful. Great for teas or anywhere you normally use honey.

INGREDIENTS

1 tbsp saffron threads
2 oz raw unfiltered honey

EQUIPMENT
spoon
glass jar with lid

PREPARATION

Add saffron to the jar. Pour in the honey, fully covering the saffron. Stir well to combine, making sure there are no air bubbles and that the stamens are fully saturated in honey.

Secure with plastic lid. Label w/ ingredients and date. Shake every other day so the honey moves and saffron stamens move.

Allow it to infuse for 4 weeks and then strain the honey through a sieve to capture the saffron stamens, then put the infused honey in a bottle.

Tip: Slowly warm the honey in a bowl of hot water, so that it softens and pours more easily when you are ready to strain.

For a calming and relaxing honey try lavender instead.

1 part lavender to 4 parts honey

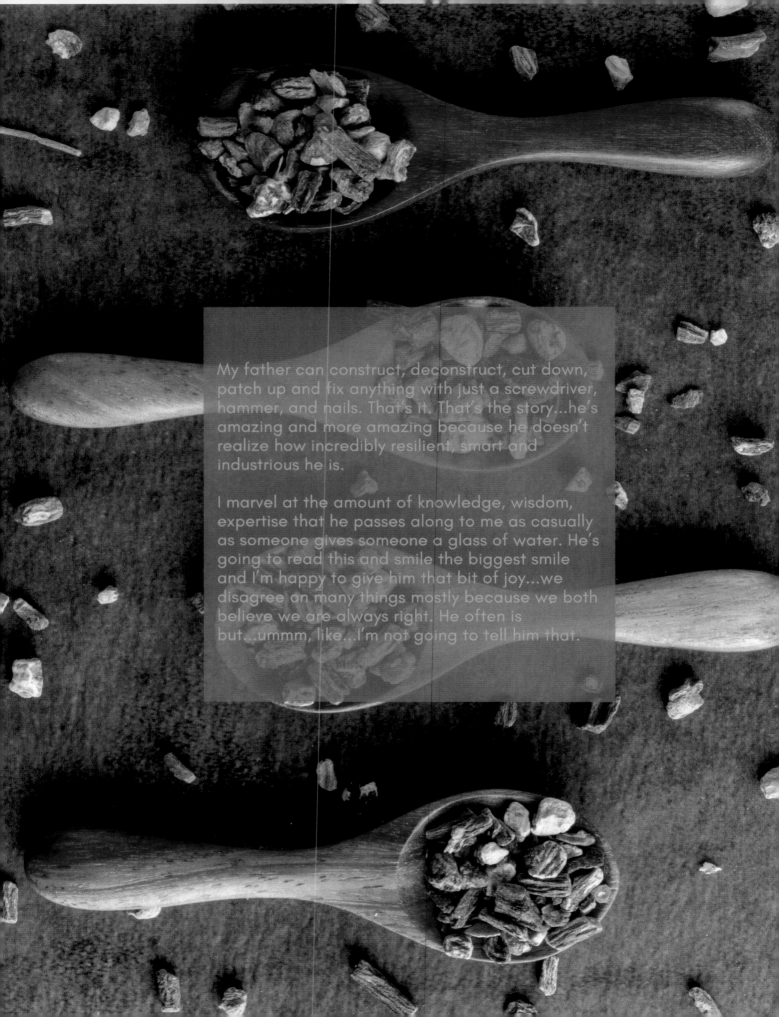

My father can construct, deconstruct, cut down, patch up and fix anything with just a screwdriver, hammer, and nails. That's it. That's the story...he's amazing and more amazing because he doesn't realize how incredibly resilient, smart and industrious he is.

I marvel at the amount of knowledge, wisdom, expertise that he passes along to me as casually as someone gives someone a glass of water. He's going to read this and smile the biggest smile and I'm happy to give him that bit of joy...we disagree on many things mostly because we both believe we are always right. He often is but...ummm, like...I'm not going to tell him that.

WILD DANDELION ROOT
TINCTURE

Dandelion moves energy, helps you to stand in your power, and tell your truth. Dandelion nourishes the gut flora by supporting digestive and gastrointestinal health. Also good in supporting your liver health and treating anemia because of dandelions high content of iron. Take 10-12 drops in water 1-3 times a day.

INGREDIENTS
2 oz dandelion root
4 oz apple cider vinegar

EQUIPMENT
4 oz glass jar with plastic lid
4 oz glass bottle with dropper top
measuring spoon
funnel
strainer or cheesecloth

Did You Know:
Shake well before use. Not for use during pregnancy or lactation. If you have a medical condition or take medications, please consult with your doctor before use.

PREPARATION
Add Dandelion root to the glass jar. Pour apple cider vinegar over the dandelion root filling the jar. Leave approx. 1/8-1/4 inch space at the top.

Secure with plastic lid. Label w/ ingredients and date. Shake every other day. Let it steep for 4-6 weeks.

Strain and pour into a tincture bottle.

Vinegar can degrade metal lids. When making vinegars or oxymels be sure to use a jar with a plastic lid. If you don't have a plastic lid, place a piece of cling wrap between the jar and metal lid before you close it.

BLACK WALNUT
EXTRACT

INGREDIENTS

3 tbsp black walnuts, shelled
1 vanilla bean
2 tbsp bourbon
vodka or glycerin

EQUIPMENT

measuringspoons
2 -2 oz or 1 - 4 oz glass
bottle with dropper top
4 oz jar with lid
fine mesh strainer or cotton
mesh sieve
cast iron skillet
spoon

PREPARATION

Pre-heat skillet on medium. Add the black
walnuts, stir for approximately 5 minutes until the
walnuts are turn a golden brown and the scent
begins to release. Set aside. Let walnuts cool;
approximately 15 minutes.

Add black walnuts, vanilla bean and bourbon into
a 4 ounce mason jar. Add vodka to fill the rest of
the jar.

Label including all ingredients and date. Shake
every other day. Let it steep for 6-8 weeks.
Strain and pour into a bottle or jar with a lid.
Label and date.

You may need to strain twice for a clearer
extract. Compost the walnuts or use in
another recipe.

**Did You
Know:**
Shake well before use. Not for use
during pregnancy or lactation. If you
have a medical condition or take
medications, please consult with your
doctor before use.

MR. GILMORE'S
WALNUT BUTTER

INGREDIENTS
1 1/2 cup raw, unsalted walnuts
1/8 tsp cinnamon

EQUIPMENT
measuring spoons and cups
baking pan
food processor
spoon

Did You Know:
Walnuts are...
Rich in Antioxidants.
Great plant source of omega-3.
Promotes a healthy gut.
Full of nutrients for optimal health.
Good source of protein, fiber and
magnesium.

PREPARATION
Add walnuts to a pan lined with parchment paper. Roast at 325°F for 12-14 minutes until they are a bit moist or slightly oily on the top.

Be mindful to not over cook we don't want to burn them.

Add roasted walnuts to food processor and for about 1-2 minutes. It should look like a chunky paste.

Roasting the walnuts brings out their natural oils, so it will process easily into a butter. Scrape down the sides and process for 1-2 minutes. It is should be oily and dripping easily as it pours off of your spoon.

LAVENDER AND
WALNUT FUDGE

INGREDIENTS

1/2 cup butter
1/2 cup sugar
1/2 cup packed light brown sugar
1/2 cup evaporated milk
1/8 teaspoon salt
1 teaspoon vanilla extract
2 cups confectioners' sugar
1 cup walnuts, lightly toasted and
coarsely chopped

EQUIPMENT

measuring spoons and cups
medium saucepan
large saucepan
baking pan
food processor
spoon

PREPARATION

In a saucepan add evaporated milk and
lavender; bring to a simmer. Remove from
heat and let steep for 10 minutes. Strain.

In a large saucepan, combine the butter,
sugars, lavender infused evaporated milk and
salt.

Bring to a boil over medium heat.

Once the mixture is boiling good, boil for 5
minutes, stirring constantley.

Remove from heat, stir in the vanilla and mix
well.

Stir in confectioner's sugar, then fold in
walnuts.

Spread mixture into a 8" square dish (the size
of the dish is not an exact, use what ever size
you desire to get the thickness you want).

Cover and let cool until room temperature.

Cut into 1 inch squares and store in airtight
container in refridgerator..

WALNUT AND FLAX
BARS

1 cup walnut butter
1/2 cup honey
1/2 cup coconut oil
1 1/2 cup oats
1/4 cup cocoa powder
1 tsp cinnamon
1/2 cup shredded coconut,
unsweetened
1/2 cup sliced walnuts
2 tbsp flaxseed

EQUIPMENT

parchment paper
food processor
spoons
measuring spoons and cups
baking pan
glass bowls
knife

PREPARATION

Add ground flax seed, oats, cocoa powder,
cinnamon, shredded coconut, and sliced
walnuts to a bowl, mix together.

Prepare a baking pan with waxed paper.
On medium heat; warm walnut butter, honey,
and coconut oil in a pan, stirring constantly
until melted and blended.

Pour hot mixture into bowl with dry
ingredients, stir until combined.

Pour into the prepared pan, chill in the fridge
for 30 mins- 1 hour. Cut into squares, store in
the fridge for up to 1 week.

NIGHTS LIKE THIS...
REVIVAL NIGHT CANDY

Revival, Church fans, Refrains of "...goin' up yonder", Grandmas with endless supply of candy for their granddaughters.

INGREDIENTS

1 cup sugar
3 tbsp corn syrup
1/2 cup water
1 tbsp rose cardamom syrup
1 tsp rosewater
2 tsp rose petals
1 tsp saffron
non-stick cooking spray

EQUIPMENT

lollipop or candy molds
measuring spoons and cup
large saucepan
candy thermometer
spoon
heatproof measuring container
with spout
candy funnel

PREPARATION

Spray lollipop molds lightly with nonstick cooking spray. Place lollipop sticks in the molds.

Combine sugar, corn syrup, and water in a large, heavy saucepan. Bring to a boil over medium-high heat.

Continue cooking until the mixture reaches 300°F, hard crack stage. Immediately remove the saucepan from heat. Let cool to about 275°.

Stir in rosewater and rose cardamom syrup. Pour the mixture into a heatproof measuring container with a spout, or a candy funnel.

Divide the mixture among your molds. Press in rose petals and saffron with a stick. Let lollipops cool and harden, about 15 minutes, before removing from the molds.

Store wrapped in cellophane bags twist tied shut, in a cool dry place for up to one month

Yield: 12 large or 24 small lollipops

This is a love that crowns the feet with hands that nourishes, conceives,
feels the water sails
mends the children,
folds them inside our history where they toast more than the flesh where
they suck the bones of the alphabet and spit out closed vowels.

This is a love colored with iron and lace.
This is a love initialed Black Genius.

This Is Not A Small Voice, Sonia Sanchez

Sweet Potato or Yam

Let's clear this up...they are not the same thing. If you are in the United States most likely what you are buying or eating is actually sweet potatoes. There are some exceptions but for the most part yams do not grow well in the United States due to climate. With all that said, let's talk about Sweet Potatoes!

I love them and grew up eating them in a variety of ways. They are delicious, nutritious, naturally sweet and are easy to grow here in Virginia. A tuberous root vegetable that take approximately 3-4 months to grow. It is usually ready to harvest just as the ends of the vines begin to turn yellow, or just before frost.

If you want to eat the leaves as greens, you can do so throughout the season but be mindful to leave enough on the plant to keep it growing.

Sweet potatoes are excellent sources of beta-carotene that when converted to vitamin A help to support your immune system and gut health. They are a rich source of fiber, antioxidants and minerals including iron, calcium, selenium.

My Favorites
-
Sweet Potato Pie
Baked Sweet Potatoes
Sweet Potato Casserole
Candied Sweet Potatoes
Sweet Potato Fries
Sweet Potato Cornbread

SWEET POTATO ICE CREAM
& WHIPPED CREAM

ICE CREAM INGREDIENTS

Dairy Included
3 large eggs
2 large egg yolks
1 1/2 cups sugar
1/2 cup brown sugar
1 cup sweet potato roasted
2 tbsp vanilla extract
1/4 tsp cinnamon
1/4 tsp nutmeg
2 cups heavy whipping cream
2 cups half and half

Non Dairy
1 large sweet potato, peeled and sliced into
1/2-inch-thick pieces
1/2 cup pure maple syrup
2 cups oat milk
1/2 cup raw honey
1 tsp pure vanilla extract
1 tsp cardamom

WHIPPED CREAM INGREDIENTS

Cardamom Whipped Cream
1/2 cup water
1/2 cup sugar
1 tbsp confectioners sugar
4-5 cardamom pods
1 cup heavy cream

Heart Warming Whipped Cream
1/2 cup water
1/2 cup sugar
1 tbsp confectioners sugar
5 whole cloves
1 tbsp cinnamon chips
1/4 tsp black peppercorn
1 star anise
1 cup heavy cream

EQUIPMENT

medium saucepan
blender or food processor
ice cream maker
medium bowl
whisk

measuring spoons and cups
pint size freezer safe container
baking dish
airtight 2 oz container

ICE CREAM

PREPARATION
All the Dairy Version

Preheat the oven to 375°F. Rub sweet potatoes with butter or oil and cover with foil before baking. Bake until very tender, without turning, for 1 hour.

Remove from the oven and store in the refrigerator for 4 hours or overnight.

Thoroughly mix sugars, cardamom, cinnamon, and nutmeg together. In a separate bowl whisk the eggs while gradually mixing in the sugar spice mixture.

Mix vanilla extract and baked sweet potato. Then add spice and egg mixture into a bowl and whisked smoothly.

Add heavy cream and half and half to a medium pot and heat to boiling level. Remove from heat.

Slowly add three tablespoons of the hot milk mixture to the egg mixture to temper it and whisk together to combine. Then slowly add in the rest of the milk mixture and continue whisk the entire time to make sure it doesn't scramble.

Pour the entire mixture into a blender and blend until the sweet potato is smooth. Place the mixture in the refrigerator for 2-3 hours to chill completely.

Add mixture to your ice cream maker and churn.

Once ice cream is done churning, add to the freezer safe container.

Freeze for at least 3-4 hours then serve. Store in the freezer when not serving. Best eaten within 3-4 days of making.

PREPARATION
Non Dairy

Preheat the oven to 375°F. Place the sweet potato into a baking dish. Pour maple syrup over top and toss until well coated. Spread in a layer and bake until very tender, without turning, for 30 minutes to 1 hour.

Remove from the oven. Refrigerate overnight to soften the sweet potato further.

In the bowl of a food processor, purée potato until creamy, about 3-4 minutes. Using a rubber spatula, scrape the bowl so the syrup doesn't settle on the bottom. Add oat milk and blend, then add honey, vanilla and cardamom. Process until mixture turns from orange to a light orange in color and becomes creamy.

Pour mixture into a 9 x 9 metal pan and freeze for 12-24 hours or until solid. Serve.

WHIPPED CREAM

PREPARATION

How to Make Whipped Cream

Note: Two options: #1 Cream and bowl must be very cold before hand beating or whisking. Option #2 Whip or hand beat cream at room temperature if you don't have time to chill.

1 cup heavy cream
2 1/2 tsp confectioners' sugar
1 tsp Herbal extract or Vanilla Extract

In a mixing bowl set in a large ice-water bath, whisk cream by hand until soft peaks form. Sprinkle with the sugar, add extract, and whisk until soft peaks return. Do not over beat.

Cardamom Whipped Cream

In a medium saucepan over medium heat, bring the water, sugar, and cardamom to a simmer, stirring to dissolve sugar; turn off heat. Strain. Let cool to room temperature.

When ready to serve, whip cream to soft peaks. Serve immediately.

Heart Warming Whipped Cream

In a medium saucepan over medium heat, bring the water, sugar, cloves, cinnamon, star anise and black peppercorns to a simmer, stirring to dissolve sugar; turn off heat. Strain. Let cool to room temperature.

When ready to serve, whip cream to soft peaks. Serve immediately.

Syrup mixtures can be strained and refrigerated in an airtight container for up to 1 week. Before using, gently reheat.

EXTRA

Vanilla Extract
Slice vanilla beans lengthwise and cover with vodka in a glass jar with a lid.
Use 1 cup of vodka for every two beans.

Seal and store in a cool place, shaking occasionally, for two months before using.

SWEET POTATO
BUTTER

For the slow cookers everywhere...time to pull out the underused small slow cooker!

INGREDIENTS

3 cups peeled sweet potatoes
(cut into slices about 1/8 to 1/4
inch thick)
1 cup unsweetened apple juice
1 tbsp molasses
1 tsp ground cinnamon
1/2 tsp ground ginger
1/4 tsp ground nutmeg
1/4 tsp ground clove
1 pinch salt
1 tbsp orange juice zest

EQUIPMENT
measuring spoons and cups
small slow cooker
hand blender
2-4 oz or an 8 oz jar with lid

PREPARATION

Combine all ingredients in a 1 or 1 ½ quart
slow cooker and stir well to combine.

Cook on low for 6-8 hours, or until the sweet
potatoes are completely cooked and soft.
Using a blender, mix everything together in
your slow cooker until smooth.

When it's done cooking, I just give it a little
whirl with my immersion blender and sweeten
to taste. You can also transfer this to a food
processor or blender for blending

Then transfer to a storage container. Store in
the refrigerator for 1 to 2 weeks.

Note: You can do this in a larger slow
cooker, but you will need to double or triple
the recipe depending on the size of your slow
cooker. Your slow cooker should be at least
half way full in order to cook the food in it
properly.

**It's easy to enjoy this with your morning coffee. Spread over a warm
biscuit or add to your hot cereal. Here are a couple more ways you can
enjoy a big batch of sweet potato butter.**

*Spread it over english muffins, waffles or pancakes.
Stir it into yogurt or smoothies.*

APPLE CIDER
MOLASSES

Sometimes all it takes is the simplest of recipes to get everone into the
kitchen. Yearly trips down to the Carolina's always began and ended with
laughter and full belly's.

INGREDIENTS

1 gallon of freshly pressed
apple cider
4 tbsp sliced fresh ginger
3 sticks of cinnamon

EQUIPMENT

heavy bottomed pot
microwavable bowl
sieve or cheesecloth
spoon
electric blender
2 pint mason jars

PREPARATION

Peel and cut out the cores of apples, dice or slice thinly 2-3 apples. Add all of them
into a bowl and cover with water. Bring the apple cider to a boil, then lower heat to
a simmer for 4 to 5 hours.

Take the soaking apples and microwave them for 4 to 5 minutes or until they begin
boiling. Remove apple peels. Puree with an electric blender.

Then strain through a sieve or cheesecloth and press out the liquid using the back of
a spoon.

Slowly, bring cider temperature back to a boil and stir in liquid. Remove from heat
and pour into a glass jar(s) with a lid.

SWEET POTATO & NUTMEG FACE MASK

Sweet potatoes can also be used to reduce acne and blackheads. As we mentioned above, sweet potatoes contain antioxidants such as Vitamin A, Vitamin C, and Vitamin E. Free radicals may cause acne and blackheads as well as acne scarring, using an antioxidant rich natural ingredient like sweet potato can be good for acne prone skin.

INGREDIENTS

1 tbsp boiled sweet potato
1 tbsp bentonite clay
1 tbsp rosewater; as needed
1/8 tsp nutmeg powder

EQUIPMENT
measuring spoons
non-metal spoon
non-metal bowl

PREPARATION

Mix the nutmeg, sweet potato, and clay of your choice together.

Add enough rosewater to the mixture until you get a paste with the consistency of ketchup. Apply the face mask and leave it on for 15 minutes.

Wash the face mask off with warm water. Follow with your daily skin care routine.

Did You Know:
Nutmeg is also an anti-inflammatory, reducing redness and inflammation. Nutmeg will exfoliate your skin by removing the top layer of dead skin to reveal a new layer of healthy, fresh skin. The exfoliation properties will also help lessen black heads and will reduce the signs of acne scars.

APPLE CIDER VINEGAR
& ROSE TONER

The role of toner in skin care is to cleanse and tighten the skin to help protect it from bacteria and other impurities. Apple cider vinegar is an astringent, which can function as a toner when applied to the skin. Its mild astringent properties help tighten the pores and gently tone the skin

INGREDIENTS

1 tsp apple cider vinegar
4 oz rose water

EQUIPMENT
glass jar withlid
4 oz glass dropper or spray bottle
cotton pads

PREPARATION

Mix apple cider with 1/2 cup rose water. Apply uniformly on the face with the help of cotton pads.

You can also store this apple cider vinegar toner in a spray bottle. Spray a light mist directly on your skin to freshen your skin throughout the day. Do not rinse it off after use.

Rose water is a gentle and fragrant natural toner. It is created by distilling rose petals with steam.

Rose water naturally low pH helps to reset your natural balance.

Rose water helps sooth, calm, and reduce skin irritations.

ETHEL MAE'S
NIGHTTIME FACE SERUM

One of my favorite parts of my day is my nightly ritual of winding down for the day before going to sleep. I remember the care, time and attention my Grandma Ethel took at cleansing and moisturizing her face every night.

INGREDIENTS

4 oz jojoba oil
3 tbsp roses
1 tbsp saffron
1 tsp oatstraw

Optional
5 drops of rose essential oil
2-3 drops of patchouli
essential oil

EQUIPMENT

4 oz glass jar with lid
measuring spoons
funnel
2 -2 oz or a 4 oz glass bottle
with eye dropper

PREPARATION

Sun Infusion

Place plant matter in a jar. Pour jojoba oil covering plant material to the top leaving approximate 1/8 to 1/4" space at the top.

Close with lid. Label w/ contents and date. Place in the sun for infusion.

Strain 4 weeks later. Use a funnel to pour oil into glass bottles. Add a label with contents, date, and usage on the bottle(s).

USE

A little goes a long way! Apply up to 4 drops to a cleansed and toned face.

Best Way to Apply

The goal is to keep your skin hydrated and protected. Apply small drops to your forehead, cheeks, chin and neck. Gently massage into your face and neck using small and gentle circular strokes with your fingertips.

SOOTHING HERBAL
BUBBLE BATH

One of my favorite but affordable and indulgent ways to practice self-care is to take a long, luxurious bath. Baths can make a serious difference when you're feeling stressed, helping you unwind after a long day at work and relax as you unwind before bed. And, the best bubble baths for adults will take your bath time ritual to a whole 'nother level.

INGREDIENTS

1 cup distilled water
4 oz organic vegetable glycerin

_____

1 tbsp castile soap
1 1/2 tbsp herbal Infused vegetable glycerin
5 drops lavender essential oil, optional

Herbal Infusion
lavender, chamomile, oatstraw & rosemary

EQUIPMENT
measuring spoons
small bowl
4 oz jar with lid

PREPARATION

Gently stir 1 tbsp castile soap, 1 1/2 tbsp herb infused glycerin and essential oils together. Add to bath under running water.

Herb Infused Vegetable Glycerin
Fill jar 1/2 way with herbs.

In a bowl, mix 3 parts organic vegetable glycerin and 1 part distilled water.

Pour liquid mixture over the herbs and filling to the top of the jar.

Label container with date, ratio of glycerine to water, and herbs used.

Shake daily for 4-6 weeks.

Strain with cheesecloth, bottle, label!

Note: If you used a fine powder you may need to double filter, and even filter through a coffee filter to ensure that no botanical material remains in your glycerite.

EXFOLIATING &
MOISTURIZING BARS

Although I've tried many times I have not been able to recreate my Grandma Ethel's cornbread. She made the best melt in your mouth buttery with a tinge of sweetness cornbread from scratch in a cast iron skillet passed down from her mother. Since I can't have her cornbread I created the next best thing. Cornmeal is a great exfoliation choice for sensitive skin. It's fine texture softens in liquid so it gently removes dead skin and absorbs excess oil without irritating delicate skin. It's the perfect exfoliation.

INGREDIENTS
1 1/4 cup cornmeal
1/4 cup walnuts
1/2 cup cocoa butter
1/4 cup shea butter
1/4 cup kidney beans, dried

EQUIPMENT
cooking spray
soap mold
spoon
measuring cup
glass bowl
coffee grinder
medium saucepan

PREPARATION
Mix the shea and cocoa butter together in the bowl.

Bring two inches of water to a boil in a saucepan and reduce the heat to low. Place the glass bowl in the saucepan to melt the ingredients, then remove from the heat.

Grind the walnuts and kidney beans in the coffee grinder. Add the cornmeal to the butter mixture, followed by the walnut bean mixture.

Stir until they're evenly distributed.
Mist your chosen mold with cooking spray and wipe clean, then pour in the mixture and let cool. Once hard, pop the bars out of the mold.

To use, rub a bar all over your body in the shower to gently exfoliate. Use within 2-3 months.

REVITALIZING HERBAL DETOX BODY WRAP

Body masks are great at creating glowing skin all over. Clarifying herbs, and clay in this wrap are excellent for toning the epidermis and stimulating your lymphatic system to remove toxins from the body

INGREDIENTS

handful of pine needles
1 tbsp lavender
2 cups water
1/4 cup french green clay
1/4 cup spirulina powder
1/2 cup epsom salt
6 drops pine essential oil

EQUIPMENT
measuring cups
small saucepan
fine-mesh strainer
medium non-metal bowl
non-metal spoon
pipette
towel or sheet
plastic wrap

PREPARATION

Measure and combine the pine needles, lavender, and water in a small saucepan. Bring the water to a boil and remove from heat.

Let the herbs infuse until the water is cool, about 30 minutes. Then filter out the herbs with a fine-mesh strainer. Set the tea to the side.

Pour the tea into a non-metal bowl. Add the clay, spirulina, and epsom salt stirring until you have a smooth paste.

Add the pine essential oils. Stir.

To apply, first line a bathtub with a towel or sheet. Then spread the mask on your body.

  Optional: Wrap each section with a piece of plastic wrap.

Cover up using the towel or sheet, and relax in the tub for 20 to 30 minutes.

Rinse off the mask in the shower and follow with a moisturizer.

Repeat 1-2 times a week. Store leftover masks in the refrigerator for up to 5 days.

STRESS MELTING
BODY BUTTER

INGREDIENTS

1/4 cup shea butter
1/4 cup coconut oil
1/4 cup kokum butter
3 tbsp magnesium oil
1 tsp argan oil
15 drops jasmine essential oil
8-10 drops bergamot essential oil
5 drops ylang ylang essential oil

EQUIPMENT

measuring cups
small heat safe glass bowl
spoon
small saucepan
pipette
hand mixer
silicone spatula
8-oz container with lid

PREPARATION

Mix shea butter, coconut oil and kokum butter to a heat-safe glass bowl or use a double boiler. Stir to mix.

Glass Bowl Method: Pour 2 inches of water into a saucepan. Bring water to a boil, then reduce the heat to low. Put the glass bowl inside the saucepan.

When the ingredients have melted, remove the bowl from the heat. Let it cool for 2-3 minutes, then stir in the magnesium oil and argan oil. Add the essential oils with a pipette.

Refrigerate the bowl for 30 minutes, then remove it and whip the cream with a hand mixer on medium for 3 to 5 minutes. Scrape down the sides with a spatula.

Transfer to a lidded container and keep it cool and dry. Use everynight before bed.

Use within 6 months.

Did You Know:

Kokum butter is highly moisturizing and rich in essential fatty acids. The fatty acids aid in softening the skin and promoting the skins elasticity. Helps to heal dry and cracked skin and improve the appearance of scars and stretch marks.

CHAI 'NILLA
BODY OIL

Almond oil is a joy from head to toe. Rich in vitamins A, B, and E, this light oil moisturizes dehydrated skin, warms tired muscles and soothes painful chapped lips and dry heels. Add in some rooibos and we have the perfect body oil to carry us into a changing season.

INGREDIENTS

1 cup sweet almond oil
3 tbsp rooibos
1 tbsp tulsi
2 tsp jasmine leaves
3 whole cloves
1 whole cardamom pod
1/2 cinnamon stick
1 vanilla bean

EQUIPMENT

measuring spoons and cup
small heat safe glass bowl or
double boiler
small saucepan
knife
spoon
fine mesh strainer or cheesecloth
2 -4 oz or a 8 oz glass bottle
with top or dropper
funnel

PREPARATION

Measure and pour the almond oil into a heat-safe glass bowl.

*If you have a nut allergy, substitute another light oil, like sunflower or grapeseed.

Use a double boiler or bring 2" of water to a boil in a small saucepan and reduce the heat to low. Then place the glass bowl inside the saucepan and gently(slowly) heat the oil.

Time to add the tulsi and rooibos which contains potent antioxidants that help to revitalize and invigorate the skin.

Measure and add the cardamom, cloves, anise, cinnamon to the almond oil. Then cut open the vanilla bean and scrape the contents into the mixture. Using vanilla beans will give you a stronger flavor and scent-- along with extra antioxidants to repair skin.

Continue to warm on low for 1 hour to infuse all the yummy ingredients, stirring occasionally with a spoon.

Remove the bowl from heat and let it cool, then filter out the tea and spices with a fine mesh strainer.

Transfer to a pretty glass bottle with a funnel. Store in a cool, dry spot.

Use
Layer on this comforting, aromatic oil as a skin moisturizer, a massage oil, or even a makeup remover.

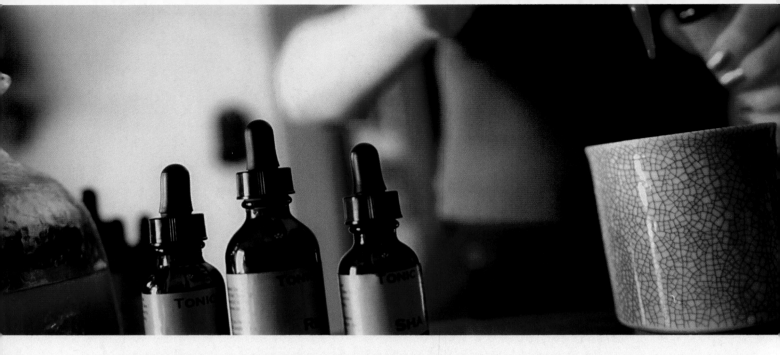

HERBAL TINCTURE & EXTRACT
SEASON REVIEW

Tinctures are liquid extractions of plant medicine, using alcohol, glycerin or vinegar as a solvent. Store jares in a cool, dark place. Shake daily for 4-6 weeks. Strain and combost the plant matter. Pour liquid into amber or blue glass droppers with tops.

Wild Dandelion Tincture
Dandelion root + Apple Cider Vinegar

Black Walnut Extract
Black Walnut + Vanilla Bean + Bourbon + Vodka or Glycerin

Fill the jar approx. 1/3 to 1/2 with roots, berries and beans. Pour menstruum to the top of the jar. Cover plants completely. The jar should appear full of herb, but herbs should move freely when shaken.

Soothing Herbal Bubble Bath
Lavender, Chamomile, Oatstraw & Rosemary + Vegetable glycerin

Fill jar approx. 1/2 to 3/4 with dried herbs. Pour vegetable glycerin to the top of the jar. Covering the plants completely.

HERBAL SALVE
SEASON REVIEW

SALVES

Peace & Quiet Sleep Balm
2 tbsp Beeswax
1 tbsp Shea Butter
3 oz Lavender, Rose, & Skullcap infused grapeseed oil
Lavender essential oil

Stress & Anxiety Release
2 tbsp Beeswax
1 tbsp Shea Butter
3 oz Lavender infused olive oil
Lavender & Neroli essential oils

DAP Hand & Foot Salve
2 tbsp Beeswax
2 tsp Kokum Butter
1 tsp Argan Oil
1 oz Magnolia infused olive oil & 2 oz Oatstraw infused olive oil
Magnolia essential oil

Pop's Don't Take No Stuff Multi-Purpose, Salve
2 tbsp Beeswax
1 tbsp Shea Butter
2 oz Black Walnut infused oil
1 oz Chamomile, Calendula & Nettle infused olive oi
Tea Tree essential oil

Don't wait until you need it to make this salve. With a shelf life of 6 months, it's a good idea to have a pot of this salve in your home, ready to bring you comfort and healing anytime.

HERBAL SALVE
SEASON REVIEW CONT'D

As Fall ushers in we begin to strain and pour the herbal oils that we've been infusing in the sun over the Summer.

EQUIPMENT
double boiler or small saucepan and glass bowl
measuring spoons and cups with pour spout
spoon
2 –2 oz or 4 oz tins with lids or wide mouthed glass container with lid

PREPARATION
Pour
Over medium heat, bring a saucepan of water to a simmer. Set a double boiler or heatproof bowl over the pot add shea butter and let it melt. Stir in infused herbal oil. Remove from heat.

Add beeswax. Stir and allow to melt over residual heat.

Pour the mixture into 2 oz or 4 oz wide mouthed containers that you can easily dip into. Let it sit on the counter for a few hours to harden.

SECTION 6

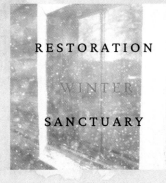

RESTORATION

WINTER

SANCTUARY

RECLAIM THE FUTURE

Winter

....is a time of restoration, music filled afternoons, hot tea, cashmere wraps and daydreams. More creating. More Laughter. More books and new authors. More hugs and new loves.

STIMULATING HAIR RINSE

PROSPERITY GREENS HAIR MASK

SAFFRON & ROSE HAIR SERUM

BID WHIST ELIXER

BLACK WALNUT EXTRACT

HAZELNUT EXTRACT

BEETROOT LEMONADE

HERBAL HOT "CAROB CHOCOLATE & HERBAL MARSHMALLOWS

RELEASE & REBUILD BEAUTY TEA

EASY LIKE SUNDAY MORNING HERBAL COFFEE

THE PAM GRIER EFFECT... LOVE & LIGHT WITH COFFY

CHAMPAGNE YUMMY GUMMIES ~ALIGN & FLOW GUMMIES~

BEETROOT ROSE GINGER SORBET

BLACK WALNUT POUND CAKE

BEETROOT CHIPS

BEET IT DYNAMC DUO ~

BODY BLUSH POWDER
BEET ROOTED(ED) CRÈME BRONZER

WATCH NIGHT PINE CLEARING SPRAY

SNOW DAYS...HYDRATION MASK

HERBAL SOLE SOAK

HAZELNUT BROWN SUGAR SCRUB

FOREST DETOX BATH

HEALING BATH TEA

ROSE & NEROLI BATH OIL

BABY IT'S SNOWING OUTSIDE BODY BUTTER

STIMULATING
HAIR RINSE

INGREDIENTS
2 tbsp lavender
1 tbsp thyme
6 cups distilled water

EQUIPMENT
1 quart jar with lid or heat
proof container with lid
medium saucepan or pot
cheesecloth
small bowl or measuring cup
measuring spoons

PREPARATION
Add herbs in a quart jar. Pour hot water
over the herbs and fill to the top. Close
with lid and steep from 30 minutes to
overnight.

Strain the herbal infusion using the
cheesecloth. You may need to strain it two
or more times to get all the plant mater
out. If some sediment remains after you've
strained don't worry about it. If you are not
using right away then label and refrerate
to keep longer.

USE
Cleanse and rinse your hair as you
normally do. Then pour the rinse over your
head and massage into your scalp.

...I am so perfect so divine so ethereal so surreal
I cannot be comprehended except by my permission...
Nikki Giovanni

PROSPERITY GREENS
HAIR MASK

Every year on New Years Eve my family does two things: Cook Greens and Black Eyed Peas, Call/Tweet/Text/Email our well wishes for a Safe, Joy-filled and Prosperous New Year to everyone we know! I like to do this hair mask before Sunrise services the next day to start my new year with a clear mind and body.

INGREDIENTS

1/4 cup sea kelp powder
1/4 cup bentonite clay
1 cup of cooled peppermint tea

EQUIPMENT
bowl
spoon
measuring cups

PREPARATION

Add sea kelp and bentonite clay to the mixing bowl and mix with a spoon. Add cooled peppermint tea and stir to form a paste.

USE
Apply paste to damp hair with fingers, rubbing into the scalp and all the way down to ends of hair. Leave on for 15-30 minutes. Rinse with warm water until the water runs clear.

This gently exfoliating and detoxifying blend with bentonite clay and seaweed cleanses environmental elements, such as dirt and pollution, and rejuvenates your hair and scalp. This mask leaves hair clean, soft, and shiny. Use twice a month or as desired. Follow with a co-wash and conditioner.

SAFFRON & ROSE
HAIR SERUM

Where there is a woman there is magic. If there is a moon falling from her mouth, she is a woman who knows her magic, who can share or not share her powers. A woman with a moon falling from her mouth, roses between her legs and tiaras of Spanish moss, this woman is a consort of the spirits.

—Ntozake Shange, Sassafrass, Cypress & Indigo

INGREDIENTS

1 1/2 tbsp saffron infused jojoba oil
1 1/2 tbsp rose infused jojoba oil
2 1/2 tbsp argan oil
1/2 tsp sea buckthorn oil, optional
2 drops rose essential oil, optional

EQUIPMENT

small funnel
measuring spoons and cup
2 oz glass bottle with dropper

PREPARATION

Combine all ingredients in a measuring cup and stir with a spoon. With funnel, pour into a glass bottle and close with eyedropper.

USE

Put a few drops into your hand, rub hands together and evenly distribute the product onto mid-shaft and ends. Add more as necessary. Works well on both damp or dry hair.

Can be used before and after styling or as an overnight treatment. Avoid storing products in direct sunlight.

Did You Know:
Sea buckthorn has high levels of essential fatty acids and vitamin A, that nourish and support scalp health. The vitamin E present in sea also helps with scalp circulation, supporting hair growth and conditioning. .

BID WHIST
HERBAL ELIXIR

Some of my clearest, warmest and happiest childhood memories were of the holidays. Playing with my cousins in a over stuffed house of relatives, a myriad of conversations, music, laughter and food. The best spot in the house was my Grandma Geraldine's kitchen where she and other realtives would be playing bid whist with a crowd of onlookers...all talking trash. I believe it was in those moments that I found my foundation for "passionate" conversation.

INGREDIENTS

4 tbsp rooibos
2 tbsp passionflower
2 tbsp roses
2 tsp damiana
2 tbsp honey
brandy

EQUIPMENT

4 oz glass jar with lid
measuring spoons

PREPARATION

Fill the jar 1/2 full with dried herbal mix. Next, fill the jar 1/2 full with brandy/menstruum and then fill the remaining half of the jar with honey. Use a spoon to mix the herbs, brandy menstruum and honey well.

Cover securely with a lid, label your jar and place in a cool, dry, dark place for 4-6 weeks. Gently shake your jar a few times a week.

Extra Loving

1 oz Bid Whist Elixir
2 oz Vodka
Ice
Orange twist

USE

Strain the herbs from your elixir and compost them. Then bottle and label your elixir. Stores up to 6 months. Enjoy in your tea, on ice or by itself.

HAZELNUT
EXTRACT

INGREDIENTS

1 cup hazelnuts, whole
2 vanilla beans
1 cup vodka
1/4 cup water

EQUIPMENT

4 oz glass jar with lid
measuring spoons
jar with sealable lid
cheesecloth and sieve
small glass bottle with lid
2 -2 oz glass bottles with dropper

PREPARATION

Preheat the oven to 375 °F. Toast the hazelnuts for 8-10 minutes.

Cut the vanilla beans lengthwise and scrape the seeds out. While the hazelnuts are still hot, transfer them into a glass jar and top with vanilla seeds. Add vodka and the vanilla beans to the jar.

Infuse for 2-4 weeks. The longer you leave it, the more intense the flavor will be. After 2-4 weeks, remove the vanilla beans and drain the hazelnuts. Reserve the extract.

Transfer the hazelnuts into a blender. Pulse 3-4 times until roughly chopped and place them into a pot. Add water and bring to boil for a minute. Remove from the heat and press the hazelnuts through a sieve, to remove any remaining fluids. Mix it with the rest of the extract.

Pour the extract through a sieve and cheesecloth to remove any pieces left. You can discard the chopped hazelnuts. If you prefer the extract clear, you can use a cheesecloth on top of the sieve to remove even the smallest pieces. Don't push it through, just let it drip slowly.

Pour the hazelnut extract into a glass jar that has been sterilized in hot water and seal well. Shake well before use just like vanilla extract. Store in the refrigerator for up to 6 months.

USE

Strain the herbs from your elixir and compost them. Then bottle and label your elixir. Stores up to 6 months.

HERBAL HOT "CAROB" CHOCOLATE
& HERBAL MARSHMALLOWS

HOT CHOCOLATE
INGREDIENTS

3 tbsp unsweetened carob powder

2 tbsp collagen powder

2 tbsp coconut powder

1 tbsp astragulus powder

1 tbsp shatavari powder

1 1/2 tsp rosehip power

1 1/2 tsp vitex, ground

raw honey, to taste

extra virgin coconut oil, optional

oat milk or milk of choice, optional

HERBAL MARSHMALLOWS
INGREDIENTS

Lavender Dreams

1 cup lavender tea

3 tbsp gelatin

1 cup raw honey

1/16 salt

1 tbsp arrowroot powder

powdered sugar

Chamomile Nights

1 cup chamomile tea

3 tbsp gelatin

1 cup raw honey

1/16 salt

1 tbsp arrowroot powder

powdered sugar

EQUIPMENT

measuring spoons and cups

small and medium saucepan

spoon

knife

whisk

electric mixer

frother

medium bowl

container with lid

9x9 baking pan

parchment paper

HOT "CAROB" CHOCOLATE
PREPARATION

Combine carob powder, collagen, coconut , astragulus, shatavari, rosehips and vitex in a bowl. Stir, mixing well. Pour into container with lid. Label and date.

USE
Stir 1-2 tbsp of carob mix and 2-3 tsp of honey into 1 cup of boiling water. Mix until smooth. This prevents any lumps if you were to place them straight in with the milk.

Option #1: Then add to the saucepan with oat milk. Bring to a slight simmer until desired temperature. Remove from heat. Pour into mug and enjoy

Option #2: Steam the oat milk. If you don't have a steamer you can warm it on the stovetop. Be sure to stir often and remove from heat just as it begins to simmer, as you don't want to scorch it.

Froth with a milk frother.

Once milk is warmed and frothed you can pour it over your herbal hot chocolate.

HERBAL MARSHMALLOWS
PREPARATION

Pour 1/2 cup herbal tea into a stand mixer. Sprinkle gelatin over the top and allow it to expand for about 10 minutes.

Add honey, salt and the remaining 1/2 cup of herbal tea to a saucepan. Heat over high heat for 8-10 minutes, until it reaches 240 degrees or soft ball stage on a candy thermometer.

When the honey syrup is up to temp, turn the stand mixer on low to break up the gelatin. Slowly pour the hot honey syrup into the stand mixer, keeping it running on low to incorporate the syrup into the gelatin.

Gradually turn up the mixer speed (to avoid splattering) and let the mixer run on high for 6-10 minutes until the marshmallow batter forms stiff peaks and is a pale white color.

Grease or line a 9x9 baking pan with parchment paper. Dust it with either a 1:1 mix of powdered sugar and arrowroot powder or choose just one. Pour the marshmallow fluff into the pan using a spatula/spatula spoon to spread the fluff throughout the pan. Sprinkle more arrowroot and powdered sugar over the top and then let the marshmallows rest for several hours or, ideally, overnight. If you live in a humid climate they you may need more time for the marshmallows to set and dry.

Store in a tightly sealed container for 1-2 days, or place in the freezer for up to 1-2 months.

To make the lavender or chamomile tea, Pour about 1 cup of hot water over herbs and allow it to steep for about 20-25 minutes. Strain.

RELEASE & REBUILD
BEAUTY TEA

INGREDIENTS
2 tbsp lavender
1 tbsp skullcap
1 tbsp peppermint
raw unfiltered honey, to taste

EQUIPMENT
airtight container
measuring spoons and cups
strainer

PREPARATION

Combine all ingredients in small bowl and stir. Store in airtight container for up to a year.

This tea is not only a powerful blend of gentle detoxifying herbs for the body and skin but it actually tastes very good. Each herb was chosen for it's distinct properties, and together they form a well balanced tea that you can drink daily.

USE
Steep 2-3 tsp in 8 oz hot water for 20-30 minutes.

MORNING HERBAL COFFEE

I learned the power of ritual through my Grandmothers. Even now I find myself daily daydreaming, re-remembering practices, prayers, time and space spent with my Grandma Ethel. Waking up early on Sunday mornings, tip-toeing towards the kitchen to catch glimpses of her sitting at the table re-applying a feisty red color to her nails while sipping her coffee.

The way the morning sunlight streamed in through the kitchen curtains and touched her skin and surrounded her felt like she was being cradled in a space of peace. There is not a morning that passes by that I don't think and remember these moments and the sense of peace they brought me.

INGREDIENTS

4 cups of water
2 tbsp dried dandelion root
1 tbsp dried burdock root
1 tsp dried chicory root
1 tsp dried astragalus root
1/4 tsp dried ginger root
1 tsp extra virgin coconut oil
milk/non dairy milk, optional

PREPARATION

Decote all ingredients in 4 cups of water for 30 minutes.

Stir in virgin coconut oil. Enjoy!

Optional
Honey and milk/non-dairy milk to taste.

EQUIPMENT
measuring spoons and cups
medium saucepan

LOVE & LIGHT WITH COFFY

There are just certain realities about our world and I just happen to be creative within it
–Pam Grier.

INGREDIENTS

1 cup oat milk
1 tsp dried ashwagandha
1 tsp dried shatavari
3/4 tsp dried rosehips
1/4 tsp cinnamon chips

EQUIPMENT

measuring spoons and cups
strainer
glass saucepan

PREPARATION

Decote ingredients in oat milk (or milk of your choice) for 30 minutes. Strain.

Pour into the Herbal Coffee recipe or enjoy on it's own..

CHAMPAGNE
YUMMY GUMMIES

Alignment and Flow. When I am looking for some balance in my life but with a fun twist I treat myself to these gummies. Yummy Tulsi helps the body adapt to stress. One of the most important benefits of tulsi tea is how it helps the body balance stress hormones, increases energy and stamina, boosting the immune system to promote a healthy metabolism while supporting healthy adrenal functions, and improving sleep.

INGREDIENTS

2 tbsp tulsi leaves
1 tbsp oatstraw
1 tsp ginger
1 1/2 tbsp saffron honey
1/16 tsp salt
4 cups of water
3 tbsp gelatin

1 cup champagne
3 tbsp gelatin
1/2 cup sugar

EQUIPMENT
measuring spoons and cup with pour spout
saucepan
silicon molds
whisk

PREPARATION

Align & Flow Gummies
Nutritive hot infusion with tulsi and ginger. Nutritive room temperature Infusion with oatstraw. In a saucepan, whisk together the tulsi ginger tea, honey and gelatin.

Let sit for 5 minutes. Then turn the heat on medium and whisk until the gelatin dissolves. Let the mixture cool to room temperature (to preserve the healthy enzymes in the raw honey) then whisk in the oatstraw tea, honey and the salt.

Remove from heat. Use a dropper or measuring cup with spout to transfer mixture into molds. Fill completely.

Place mold in refrigerator for 1-2 hours or until gummies are completely firm.

Gently remove each gummy from the mold.

Champagne Gummies

Combine champagne, gelatin, and sugar in a large saucepan over medium heat, and stir until the gelatin has completely dissolved.

Note: Do not allow your mixture to reach a boiling point or even a low simmer or you will cook out all of the alcohol.

Remove from heat. Use a dropper or measuring cup with spout to transfer mixture into molds. Fill completely.

Place mold in refrigerator for 1-2 hours or until gummies are completely firm.

Gently remove each gummy from the mold.

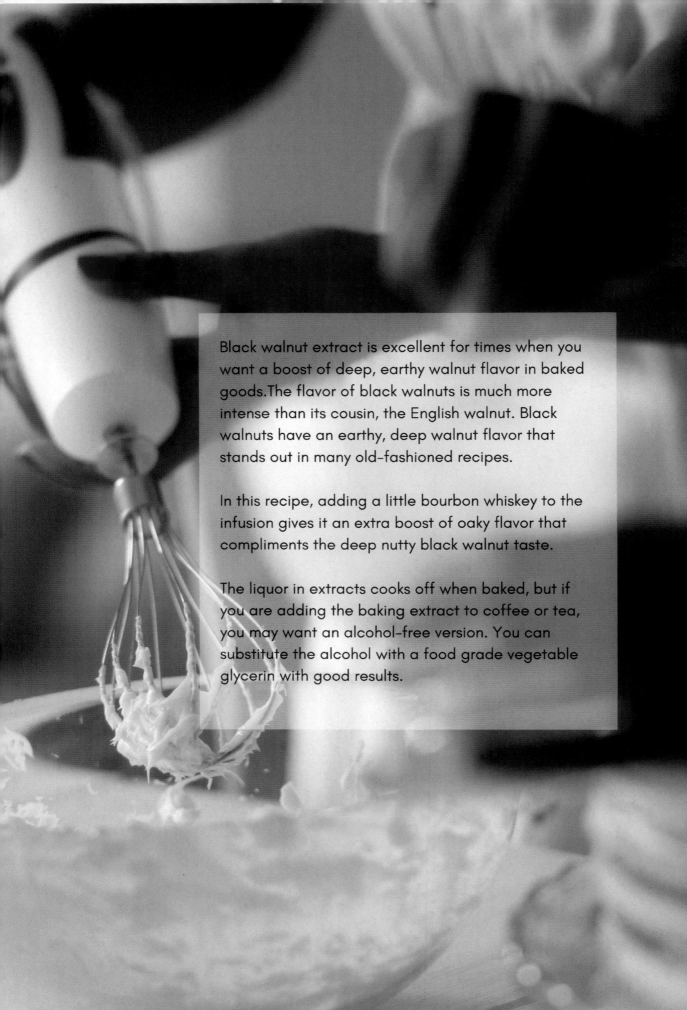

Black walnut extract is excellent for times when you want a boost of deep, earthy walnut flavor in baked goods.The flavor of black walnuts is much more intense than its cousin, the English walnut. Black walnuts have an earthy, deep walnut flavor that stands out in many old-fashioned recipes.

In this recipe, adding a little bourbon whiskey to the infusion gives it an extra boost of oaky flavor that compliments the deep nutty black walnut taste.

The liquor in extracts cooks off when baked, but if you are adding the baking extract to coffee or tea, you may want an alcohol-free version. You can substitute the alcohol with a food grade vegetable glycerin with good results.

BLACK WALNUT
POUND CAKE

INGREDIENTS

2 cups of unbleached all-purpose flour
1 1/2 cups of sugar
5 eggs
1 1/2 cups of butter
1/4 cup of milk
2 tsp black walnut and vanilla extract
1 tsp salt
1 cup chopped black walnuts

EQUIPMENT

2-3 bowls needed
electric mixer
wooden spoon
tube cake pan

Did You Know:
Nearly all Black Walnuts come from trees growing in the wild, while English walnuts come from orchards.

The main difference between Black Walnuts and English walnuts are the rich, bold, distinctive flavor of the Black Walnut. Black Walnuts are a nutritional nuts containing the highest protein content of any tree nut.

Black walnuts have higher levels of antioxidants, polyunsaturated fatty acids, and other health-promoting compounds than the more common English walnuts, making them useful in reducing the risk of cancer, heart disease, and diabetes.

PREPARATION

If you are straining your extract at this time; include them in the recipe.

Heat in skillet over medium heat. Add the black walnuts and stir frequently until the walnuts are fragrant and golden brown, about 5 minutes.

Mix flour and baking powder. Set to the side.

Put the butter in a mixing bowl, and beat on medium speed until the butter becomes waxy. Add the sugar gradually. Beat until the mixture becomes white and light in texture.

Drop in one whole egg at a time, beating after each addition. Mix in half of the flour, then add salt and black walnut vanilla extract, (milk) and beat again.

Add the rest of the flour, mix thoroughly, then add the black walnuts and mix well again.

Butter and flour the bottom of a 9-inch tube pain, and spoon the batter into it. (Bake at 325 degree F for 50 minutes) at which time the cake should have risen to the top of the pan and become brown.

Remove from the oven and cool in the pan on a wire rack for 15 minutes. When cooled store in a tin lined with wax paper.

BEET ROOT
LEMONADE

INGREDIENTS

1 cup freshly squeezed lemon juice
1/2 cup freshly squeezed beet juice, or 2 medium-sized beets, peeled and cut into cubes
1/2 cup honey
6 cups water
ice, for serving

EQUIPMENT

pitcher
food processor
measuring cup
large bowl
spoon

PREPARATION

Making Beet Juice:
Use shredding blade on a food processor and shred the beet cubes.

This would make about 1 cup of shredded beets.

Add 4 cups of water and process until smooth.

Strain beet mixture through a sieve into a large bowl, pressing with the back of a spoon to extract as much liquid as possible.

Making Lemonade:
Add beet juice, lemon juice, honey and 2 cups of water into the pitcher. Stir well and then taste.

Adjust the sweetness, tartness, or water levels to taste. Place in the fridge until well chilled.

To serve, pour the lemonade over a glass of ice cubes. Enjoy!

BEETROOT ROSE
GINGER SORBET

INGREDIENTS

3 beets
1 cup rose tea, cooled
1/2 cup granulated sugar
Zest of 1 orange
1/2 tsp fresh ginger
3 small sprigs fresh thyme
1 cup freshly squeezed orange juice
1 1/2 tbsp honey
1/4 tsp cinnamon

EQUIPMENT

medium saucepan
measuring spoons and cups
blender
medium mixing bowl
freezer-safe container with lid
whisk
ice cream maker
shallow freezer-proof pan
strainer

To Freeze without a Machine

Place sorbet in a shallow freezer-proof pan. Allow to almost freeze fully (1 to 1 1/2 hours), and stir the mixture completely. Repeat the freeze/stir process a two more times to ensure a consistent texture (this breaks up ice crystallization).

PREPARATION

Peel and chop beets into small pieces.

Peel and dice fresh ginger.

In a medium saucepan combine the beets, rose tea, sugar, orange zest, ginger, and thyme over medium heat. Reduce the heat to low, and simmer for 20 to 30 minutes, until the beets are tender. Cover and allow to sit and cool for 10 minutes.

Using a fine mesh strainer over a mixing bowl, pour the mixture through. Add the strained liquid and beet pieces into a blender. Blend until the mixture is a smooth puree texture.

Place beet puree into a sealed container and refrigerate for 1-3 hours until it has fully cooled .

Combine the fresh orange juice, honey and cinnamon in a small saucepan over low heat.

Whisk just until the honey dissolves. Remove from heat and place in a covered container in the refrigerator for 1 hour. and remove from heat. Place in a covered container and chill in the refrigerator.

When both mixtures are completely chilled, add them together and whisk to fully combine.

Ice Cream Maker

Process the liquid in an ice cream maker following the manufacturer's instructions. Once sorbet is fully frozen in the machine, remove and place in a freezer-safe container to chill overnight for best consistency.

BEETROOT
CHIPS

So...I love potato chips and beets so beetroot chips was inevitable. I created this recipe as a way keep my crunchy habit on hand but in a way that taste good and keeps me healthy.

INGREDIENTS

12 beets
1/2 cup olive oil
2 tsp sea salt

EQUIPMENT

large bowl
oven
knife
parchment paper
baking sheets
veggie brush
air fryer

PREPARATION

Thinly slice beets to approx. 1 1/16" into a large bowl. Mix in oil and sea salt.

The oil coats the beets in preparation for baking, while the salt seasons and sweats the moisture out of the beets. Removing some of the water in the beets makes a difference in their color, size and crunch.

After 20-25 minutes, the beets have released their excess moisture and are ready for baking in low heat

Preheat the oven to 325 degrees F, and line several baking sheets with parchment paper. Scrub the beets well with a veggie brush and cut off the tops.

BEETROOT
CHIPS CONTINUED...

Toss the beets again, then drain off the liquid. Lay the slices out in a single layer on the prepared baking sheets. Bake for 45-60 minutes until crisp, but not brown. Test after 45 minutes and only bake longer if necessary. Remove the beet chips from the oven and cool completely before storing in an air-tight container.

Option #2
Air Fryer...I know there are a lot of Air Fryer Lovers out there!

- 3 medium-size red beets, peeled and cut into 1/8-inch thick slices (about 3 cups slices)
- 2 teaspoons canola oil
- 3/4 teaspoon kosher salt
- 1/4 teaspoon black pepper

Toss sliced beets, oil, salt, and pepper in a large bowl.

Place half of the beets in an air fryer basket, and cook at 325°F until dry and crisp, 27-30 minutes, shaking the basket every 5 minutes. Repeat with remaining beets.

BODY BLUSH POWDER

There is always some beauty in life. Look up ... and get on with it. Build you a
rainbow. Do it yourself! If you can't do that, build your mind near one. Learn
how to fly. Then ... soar a little.

— J. California Cooper, Some Love, Some Pain, Sometime: Stories

INGREDIENTS

1 tbsp arrowroot powder
1 tbsp beetroot powder
1 tbsp cocoa powder
1 tbsp hibiscus powder

EQUIPMENT
measuring spoons
mixing bowl
container with lid

PREPARATION

Mix together arrowroot powder, hibiscus powder
and beetroot powder.

Adding and mixing the cocoa powder gradually,
testing and adjusting the color until desired shade
is reached.

Place in container with a lid.

BEETROOT(ED)
CRÈME BRONZER

Subtly Bold and Versatile.

The benefit of a crème blush is that it stays longer and can be much bolder and more versatile than powdered blush.

Try using a makeup brush to apply but you can also use your fingers.

INGREDIENTS

1 tbsp shea butter
1 1/2 tsp emulsifying wax
1 3/4 tbsp aloe gel
1-2 tsp cocoa powder
1 tsp beetroot powder
1 tsp hibiscus powder
1 tsp mica powders (of choice)

PREPARATION

Melt shea butter and emulsifying wax in a double boiler until completely melted.

Add the aloe and whisk until completely incorporated and smooth. Remove from heat.

Slowly, start mixing the cocoa, beetroot, hibiscus, and mica powders into a heated mixture until you achieve the color that you like. Experiment with the colors until you get the desired shade. It will look much darker while making it than it will on the skin.

Notes:
For a thicker and longer lasting bronzer just add more wax when using the aloe. It will also make a smoother and more subtle mix.

For a more rose color blush add more reddish mica powders. Adding more cocoa powder or bronze mica will create a richer bronzer.

Why Should You Make Your Own Herbal Body-Care Products?
They're less expensive than those you purchased in the store. They can be made to suit your body's specific needs. These are not one-size-fits-all products! The basic recipes can be amended to fit your body's specific needs.

You get to choose what goes into the products, so there are no unknown factors involved.
Many of the oils, vinegars, and herbs the recipes require are probably already in your kitchen.

Making your own body-care products can be fun. You'll find that once you start making them, you'll be hooked. Most importantly you can use ingredients already on your shopping list or growing in your backyard

WATCH NIGHT
PINE CLEARING SPRAY

Clearing Spray, Smudge Spray, Room Clearing, Pine,
Have you ever wanted to clear and cleanse a location but don't want the smell of smoke? Ideal for clearing, cleansing and rejuvenating personal or office spaces and your being.

INGREDIENTS

distilled water
pine needles

EQUIPMENT

still
glass bowl (receiver)
vegetable steamer
filter paper
funnel
glass jars or glass spray
bottles

PREPARATION

Pour 3 quarts of water in the pot still. Mix in 10 oz of Pine Needles or cover the bottom with a layer of pine needles. Let it sit and infuse for 2-3 hours.

Remove the center post from a metal veggie steamer basket and stand the steamer, spread fully opened, in the center of the pot. Place the receiver bowl on the center of the steamer.

Put the lid right side up on the still. Bring to a boil. When water begins to simmer; reduce heat to low/medium. Heat should be high enough to maintain the vaporization of the liquids. Turn the lid upside down on the pot/still.

Place bags full of ice on the lid. Inside the pot or still, the vapor will rise to the cooler lid, condense back to liquid, flow down to the low point of the lid, and drip into the receiver. The receiver will collect the hydrosol and volatile oil. Beware of steam whenever lifting the lid of the pot.

Place a wetted filter paper in a funnel. Place the funnel into a jar or glass spray bottle.

When the hydrosol is cool, pour it through the filter paper. The hydrosol will pass through; if any significant volatile oil is present, it will collect in the bottom of the filter paper. You can collect this volatile oil with a dropper bottle pipette.

Cap the jar or spray bottle. Label with content, date, and refrigerate.

USE

Spray anywhere in the house, office, car or on yourself.

SNOW DAYS...
HYDRATION MASK

INGREDIENTS

2 tsp calendula flowers powder
2 tsp oatstraw powder
1 tbsp coconut milk powder
1 tbsp collagen powder
argan oil
water

EQUIPMENT

measuring spoons
blender or spice grinder
small bowl
washcloth

PREPARATION

Create your own herbal powder
Add calendula and oatstraw into a blender or spice grinder. Grind into a powder.

Add the coconut milk and collagen powders, and pulse again in the blender to combine all of the ingredients.

USE

Scoop out 1 tbsp of powder and add it to a small bowl. Drizzle droplets of water over the powder and stir to activate the mask, adding enough water to form a creamy paste.

You can also add one or two drops of argan oil for extra moisture for your skin. Apply the mask to your skin and let it sit for 15 minutes, then remove with a dampened washcloth.

I like to remove my masks in the shower, so that it doesn't make a mess.

GOLDEN SOUL
FACE BALM

INGREDIENTS

4 tbsp shea butter
2 tblsp cocoa butter
1 1/2 tsp beeswax
2 tbsp calendula infused
jojoba oil
1 tbsp comfrey infused jojoba oil
1/4 tsp vitamin E
1/4 tsp sea buckthorn oil
15 drops jasmine or neroli
essential oil, optional

EQUIPMENT

bowl
spoon
2 -2 oz or a 4 oz glass jar with
lid or tin with lid

PREPARATION

Heat approx. 2 inches of water in small pot into a simmer. Place double boiler over the pot.

Add shea butter, cocoa butter, beeswax to double boiler. When fully melted, remove from heat. Wait until it is lukewarm to touch, and pour into mixing bowl with remaining ingredients. Stir well with spoon. Pour into jar with lid. Let cool for 2-3 hours before using.

USE

Use with dry, clean fingers, morning and night as moisturizer or as needed. If stored out of direct sunlight, will keep for up to a year.

Did You Know:

Sea buckthorn is one of several antioxidant-rich oils that come together in this protective and hydrating face oil that's great for any and all skin types.

HERBAL SOLE
SOAK

INGREDIENTS
1/2 cup sea salt
1/2 cup epsom salt
1 1/2 tbsp baking soda
1 tbsp peppermint leaves
6 cups water

EQUIPMENT
measuring spoons and cup
bowl

PREPARATION
For Comfort or Relaxation
Add water to pot, additional ingredients, stir and bring to a boil. Remove from heat.

Let water cool and transfer to a container large enough to soak feet in.

Dancers Foot Soak
1 tbsp Chamomile + 1 cup Epsom Salt

Errand Day Foot Soak
1 tbsp Chamomile + 2 tbsp Rose
1 cup Himalayan Pink Salt
10 drops Rose essential oil
5 drops Neroli essential oil

Release the Day Foot Soak
1 tbsp Lavender + 1 tbsp Skullcap
1 cup Epson Salt
10 drops Patchuli essential oil

HAZELNUT
BROWN SUGAR SCRUB

INGREDIENTS
1 cup light brown sugar
1/4 cup coconut oil
1 tbsp ground coffee
1 tsp hazelnut extract, optional

EQUIPMENT
measuring spoons and cup
bowl
6 oz swing top glass jar

PREPARATION
In a small bowl add coconut oil and brown sugar. Mix until soft scrub forms.

Add coffee grounds and repeat.

Pour in optional hazelnut extract.

Spoon into airtight containers and store for up to one month.

USE
Apply the body scrub in the shower first before you later up with soap.

*Use this exfoliating scrub on your skin in the morning for an extra boost of energy.

FOREST DETOX
BATH

INGREDIENTS

1 cup of pine needles or 20 drops of pine essential oil
1 cup sea salt
1 cup epsom salt
2 tsp bentonite clay
1/4 cup spirulina powder
1/4 cup kelp powder

EQUIPMENT
measuring spoons and cup
16 oz jar with lid
bowl
spoon

PREPARATION

Mix all ingredients together in a bowl and stir well. Spoon into a jar and close with lid.

Use 1/4 to 1/2 cup per bath or as desired. Will keep fresh up to a year.

This green bath will envelop your senses and balance your body. Nourishing kelp stimulates blood flow and draws impurities out of skin.

Antioxidant-rich spirulina fight free radicals, retains moisture, and creates a beautiful jade-green hue over the bath. Epsom salt relieves tired muscles and eliminates toxins, while mineral-rich sea salt balances skin moisture and improves circulation.

By harvesting the aromatic needles you can get many of the benefits of it's is rich health boosting actions to relieve pain, soothe inflammation, and get you feeling better faster. Make some now to have on hand when you need it during the cold and flu season.

IT'S ALWAYS A GOOD TIME
FOR A HEALING BATH

Herbal Bath Three Ways...

Option #1

INGREDIENTS

1 cup sea salt
dried herb(s)
32 oz water

EQUIPMENT

large pot with lid
strainer
measuring spoons and cups

PREPARATION

Fill pot with 32 oz of water and bring to a boil. Remove from heat.

Add herb(s), cover with lid and steep for 30 minutes. Strain.

Draw a warm bath. Once bath is ready add 1/4 cup of sea salt and pour the strained medicinal bath tea into the tub. Enjoy the bath for 15-20 minutes.

Option #2

INGREDIENTS

dried herbs
essential oil

EQUIPMENT

measuring spoons and cup
small muslin bag or piece of cheesecloth and string

PREPARATION

Place herbs into the muslin bag.

If using cheesecloth, place herbs in the center of the cloth, gather up the edges, and tie with string.

Tie or hook herbal tea bag over the faucet as the bath fills, allowing water to run through the bag or cheesecloth.

Once filled, remove the tea bag from the faucet and let it steep in the water as you soak.

Enjoy the aroma and healing properties.

Option #3

To use this recipe add 1 cup of bath tea to a cotton muslin bag with the drawstring tightly drawn.
   Add the bag to the bathtub while it fills with warm water.
   Allow the bath tea to infuse the water,
   After bath is finished running or bath is complete compost the used herbs.
   Rinse and dry the cotton muslin bag to reuse.

TEA

Tipping Out the Tea House
Soothes tired muscles, skin and mind
1 1/2 tbsp Lemon Balm + 1 1/2 Peppermint
+ 5 drops Tea Tree oil

Juke Joint Dreams
Calms frazzled nerves
1 tbsp Lavender + 1 tbsp Rose + 1 tbsp Calendula

Sleep Easy
Relieves insomnia and dry itchy skin
2 tbsp Chamomile + 1 tbsp Skullcap + 1 tbsp Nettles

Breathe Free
Helps to relieve congestion
2 tbsp Eucalyptus

ROSE & NEROLI
BATH OIL

Bath oils are wonderful, especially if you have dry or sensititve skiin. Comforting carrier oils, along with aromatic essential oils, will protect and richly moisturize the skin.

INGREDIENTS

3 oz rose infused olive oil
3 tbsp argan oil
10 drops rose essential oil
5 drops neroli essential oil

EQUIPMENT

measuring spoons and cup
4 oz glass bottle with dropper top
small funnel

PREPARATION

Using a funnel pour rose infused olive oil and argan oil in the bottle. Add essential oil. Shake, mixing well.

Note: Bath oils can be very concentrated and slippery. Be careful getting in and out of the tub.

USE

Fill bath with warm water and pour 1-2 tbsp of oil in right before you are ready to get in.

BABY IT'S SNOWING OUTSIDE
BODY BUTTER

Just what your skin needs for the winter months. Thicker and richer than body cremes, body butters are highly concentrated formulas that are not as easily absorbed as lotions or creams. They are best suited to super-dry skin where a barrier cream is required.

INGREDIENTS

1/2 cup shea butter
1/4 cup cocoa butter
1/4 cup of rose saffron infused oil
20 drops neroli essential oil

EQUIPMENT

measuring spoons and cup
widemouthed jar with lid
bowl
spoon
handheld blender

PREPARATION

In a bowl, add the shea and cocoa butters. Blend with a handheld blender and then drizzle in the herbal infused oil. Add the essential oil and continue blending for 3-5 minutes, until smooth.

Put the body butter in a widemouthed jar. You can also pipe it into your jar if you want to have a buttercream like swirl at the top.

USE

Apply body butter all over, especially in any areas that need extra moisturizing attention. It's best to apply the body butter onto damp skin, right after a shower. It will absorb very quickly and leave you feeling soft and smooth.

Body Butters are all about feel-good indulgence. Our skin is a sense organ, which means the experience that skin care provides on the outside can make a big difference in the way you feel on the inside. Here, solid butters are whipped into an airy with a soothing texture that feels like being wrapped in the coziest blanket.

Seasonal PRACTICE

YEAR:

INTENTION:

MONTH	GOALS
January	
February	
March	
April	
May	
June	
July	
August	
September	
October	
November	
December	

Rich Red Clay Soil
Poke Sallat
High John the Conqueror
Mountain Ranges & Ocean Views
Spoon Bread
Cast Iron Skillets
Deep Freezers

Riding on the Back of Pick-up Trucks
Peanut Farms
Corn Liquor
Paw Paw Trees
Virginia Ham

Sweet Corn
Tobacco
Whole Hog BBQ

Apricot Wine
Fried Apples and Biscuits

Butter Rolls and Ham
Ports and Trade Routes

SECTION 9

THE GOOD STUFF

PREPARATION WITH PURPOSE

ACTIONS OF HERBS

Adaptogens: An herb that improves the body's ability to adapt, helping it to adapt around a problem. It helps the body to avoid reaching a point of collapse or over stress.

Alterative: Herbs that will gradually restore the proper function of the body and increase health and vitality. They were at one time known as "blood cleansers". It alters the body over time.

Analgesic/Anodyne: Analgesics are herbs that reduce pain and are either applied externally or taken internally.

Antiemetic: Can reduce a feeling of nausea and can help to relieve or prevent vomiting. Ex. Seasickness, pregnancy.

Anti-inflammatory: Herbs that help the body combat inflammations

Antispasmodic: Herbs can prevent or ease spasms or cramps. Ex.) PMS, sports injuries.

Aperients: Herbs that are very mild laxatives.

Aromatic: Herbs that have a strong and often pleasant odor which can stimulate the digestive system. They are often used to add aroma and taste to other medicines.

Astringent: Contracts tissue by precipitating proteins and can thus reduce secretions and discharges. They contain tannins. Ex.) hemorrhaging or diarrhea

Bitter: Herbs that taste bitter and act as stimulating tonics for the digestive system through a reflex via the taste buds. Helps us to process and break down our food.

Cardiac Tonic: Cardiac tonics affects the heart.

Carminative: Rich in volatile oils and by their action, stimulate the peristalsis of the digestive system and relax the stomach, thereby supporting the digestion and helping against gas in the digestive tract. Ex.) spicy herb, chamomile, ginger, peppermint.

Cholagogue: Stimulate the release and secretion of bile from the gallbladder. They can also have a laxative effect on the digestive system since bile is internally produced. It is an all-natural laxative.

Demulcent: Rich in mucilage and can soothe and protect irritated or inflamed internal tissue. For ex.) a sore throat

Diuretic: Increases the secretion and elimination of urine.

Emollient: Applied to the skin to soften, soother, and protect it. They act externally in a manner similar to the way demulcents act internally.

Hepatic: Aids the liver. They use tones and strengthen it and increase the flow of bile. Bile is what the liver produces to cleanse the colons (to push waste out of the body).

Hypnotic: Will induce sleep (not a hypnotic trance). Ex.) valerian

Laxative: Promotes the evacuation of the bowels.

Nervine: Has a beneficial effect on the nervous system to tone and strengthen it. Some act as stimulants, some as relaxants. Stimulants: for depression.   Relaxants: Anxiety. Important to know the difference

Rubefacient: When applied to the skin they can cause a gentle local irritation to stimulate the dilation of the capillaries, thus increasing circulation to the skin. Blood is drawn from deeper parts of the body into the skin and thus often internal pains are relieved.

Sedative: Calms the nervous system and reduces stress and nervousness throughout the body. They can thus affect the tissue of the body that has been irritated by nervous problems.

Soporific: Induces sleep. Makes you sleepy.

Stimulant: Quicken and enliven the physiological functions of the body.

Styptic: Reduces and stops bleeding by their astringency. Ex.) Internal and external bleeding (mostly internal)

Tonic: Strengthens and enlivens either specific organs or the whole body. Use daily/ all the time =must be consistent with this.

Vulnerary: Are applied externally and aid the body in the healing of wounds and cuts.

HERBAL PREPARATIONS

Infusion
An infusion is a quantity of fresh or dried herbs steeped in freshly boiled water. This process is used to prepare delicate parts of plants, such as leaves and flowers. Use a glass or enamel container, distilled water, or good water/spring water.

Standard Infusion
1 teaspoon dried herb per cup of water, steep for 20 minutes.

Nutritive Infusion
1/4 cup of herbs to 1 cup of water, steep for 20-40 minutes and/or overnight.

Decoction
This method is used for the harder parts of the plant, such as roots, bark, and seeds. 1 tablespoon per 1 1/2 - 2 cups of water, bring to a boil then simmer at low heat for approximately 30 minutes.

Iced Tea
Prepared the same way as hot tea. Cool in the refrigerator.

Sun-Lunar Tea
A sun or lunar tea is used to capture the energy of the sun (yang, heating) or the moon (yin, cooling). Fill a clear gallon jar with distilled water or "good water". Add 1 cup of herbs of your choice, set in sun or moonlight for approx. 4-6 hours. You can also use colored jars, introducing Color therapy. Add sweetener or juice. Be creative; put affirmations or crystals on your jars.

Average Shelf Life of Herbal Tea
Keeps for 3 days in the refrigerator

Menstruums/Solvents
A menstruum/solvent is a substance that can be infused with the healing properties of herbs. Examples include water, oils, alcohol, honey, and glycerin.

Nectar of Life=Water

Water. Every part of our body depends on water. The human body can live four or five days at the most with out water. Water protects our joints and organs; especially our kidneys and colon in helping to flush toxins out of the body. A water medium is used to most actions in the body. Our bodies need water when we get hot to produce sweat. This sweat evaporates and cools our bodies down.

Types of Oils

Almond Oil (cold-pressed)
Light and nearly odorless and good for most skin types. It's often mixed with more emollient oils and is especially good at softening the skin when used in creams and lotions.
Note: I use only cold-pressed almond oil in my recipes.

Argan Oil (cold-pressed Moroccan)
One of my favorite oils. Argan oil is anon-greasy and absorbs quickly, visibly brightening and softening the skin. It contains many vitamins and fatty acids. It's absorbed quickly and is especially good for damaged, severely dry and aged skin. Can be used to make amazing hot-oil treatments for damaged, brittle hair.

Coconut Oil (raw, virgin and unrefined)
Made from pressing raw coconut meat, the oil, which smells like fresh coconut, is a sumptuous moisturizer for skin and hair. It has the ability to strengthen skin tissues, improve elasticity. It is high in antioxidants and vitamin E, as well as fatty acids, including lauric acid, a natural microbial. It is often used in both solid and liquid soaps for its ability to produce a lovely lather.

Grapeseed Oil (expeller pressed)
This is one of the lightest oils out there (and my favorite). Great carrier oil in perfumes and scented body-care recipes. It absorbs quickly into the skin, I love to use it in lotions and creams because it's smooth but not greasy.

Note: Grapeseed oil can be extracted with solvents that are bad for the skin. You should use the expeller pressed kind in your recipes.

Jojoba (cold-pressed, and unrefined)
This oil is made from the seeds of the Simmondsia chinensis (jojoba) plant, technically, it isn't an oil—it's a liquid plant wax. When applied it acts as a second skin, providing protection and emollience while allowing the skin to breathe.

Olive (extra virgin olive oil; cold-pressed and unrefined)
Can be used alone or in combination with other oils. Great for dry and sensitive skin and helps to reduce the appearance of scars and aged skin.

Cocoa Butter (unrefined)
Made from the fat that's extracted from cocoa beans, this oil has a heavenly chocolate scent. It's solid at room temperature, but melts when applied to the skin. I use it as an emulsifier and stiffener in creams. It's very protective and helps keep the skin hydrated.

Shea Butter (virgin and unrefined)
High in vitamins A, E, and F; provides collagen and is a natural emollient. It has a natural SPF of 6. This butter helps with skin elasticity. Virgin, unrefined shea butter has a mild nutty smell and is soft at room temperature.

Side Note: It is made from the nuts of the shea (karite) tree in Africa. The shea tree (Vitellaria paradoxa) is indigenous to Africa and grows in parkland agroforestry systems across the Sahel. The shea trees grow in a narrow belt of fertile, well-drained soils in the savannah, stretching from West Africa to East Africa.

Honey
External
A mild antiseptic, making it a great for treating wounds, scrapes, and burns. It's anti-inflammatory properties help reduce pain and swelling from injuries.

Internal
Uused internally to help with chronic fatigue, increase energy, and improve the immune system. It's calming effects promote sleep. It is naturally emollient, humectant, antibacterial, and full of antioxidants.

Use raw, unpasteurized, and local honey when possible.

Beeswax
A natural wax produced by honeybees. It's a great thickener for salves, creams, lip balms, and lotions. It has preservative and antibacterial properties, which can help extend the shelf life of body care products.

Salt
Salt contains minerals that are nourishing and is very therapeutic for the skin and hair. It's drawing and detoxifying; excellent as an exfoliator and cleanser. Removes toxins, dirt, and dead cells, leaving clean and soft skin and hair cleaner.

There are many different types and colors of salt. Some of my favorites are listed below.

Black Lava Salt
A sea salt that's been mixed with activated charcoal and contains many trace minerals It's an amazing black-gray color and very detoxifying.

Sea Salt
Sea salt is produced when seawater evaporates. Cleansing, drying and abrasive it's great for baths, scrubs, and foot soaks.

Use unprocessed sea salt because it contains more minerals and will be more therapeutic.

Pink Salt
The color of the salt is caused by its high iron content. Pink salt has a very high percentage of minerals (it contains more than 80 different kinds), which makes it very nourishing for the body. It's very effective at dispelling toxins and it's great for treating skin issues like psoriasis, eczema and rashes.

Epsom Salt
Not really salt! It's a chemical compound that contains magnesium, sulfur, and oxygen. It has often been used for cosmetic purposes. It's prized for its therapeutic, anti-inflammatory properties, which make it helpful for reducing muscle soreness and drawing toxins from the body.

Clay

Bentonite
This soft, mucilaginous clay results from the weathering of volcanic ash. It's mild and good for all skin types, especially problem skin. I find it to be very healing.

Green Clay
Sometimes also called sea clay, it contains high concentrations of decomposed plant material, which give it a green color. It's mild and compatible with most skin types.

Red Clay
The iron in this clay gives it a distinctive rust color. Extremely detoxifying, red clay is a drying, drawing substance, which makes it perfect for people with acne, oily complexions or problem skin. I like to use this clay in treatments for poison ivy and poison oak. It's my favorite clay to use in face and body masks.

Kaolin
Kaolin, also known as white clay and is the least of the drying clays. It is mild and well suited for dry or sensitive skin but good for all skin types.

Other Common Preservatives

Activated Charcoal (or activated carbon)
Is used both externally and internally to detoxify skin and body. Abie to draw out dirt, impurities, pollution, and chemicals so you can wash them away. It is great for all skin types but particularly oily skin. It is perfect in a cleanser or face mask.

Apple Cider Vinegar
It is anti-inflammatory and astringent, and it helps to balance the pH of your skin.

Castile soap
A natural cleanser made by turning into soap, plant oils such as olive oil, coconut, sunflower, and jojoba, with the addition of potassium hydroxide. It is great for washing face, body, and hair and can be used in household cleaners.

Vitamin E
Helps prevent oil-based body products from going rancid. High in antioxidants that repair and protect the skin.

Vegetable Glycerin
Has a sweet and syrup-like consistency. It's often substituted for alcohol in extract and tinctures. It's an emollient and hydrating for the skin. It draws moisture from the air by pulling moisture up from the lower layers of skin to hydrate the skin.

Alcohol/Spirits (Vodka, Brandy, Bourbon)
I use alcohol when I'm making an elixir, extract or tincture, I typically use brandy or vodka.

Witch Hazel
A natural astringent distilled from the leaves and bark of the witch hazel tree. Used to disinfect and treat skin irritation. Important in any natural first-aid kit.

Hydrosols

Hydrosols are a by-product of steam distillation. When you distill plant material to make essential oils, you are left with oil floating on top of water. The essential oils are separated out, and the leftover water is beautifully infused with the plant essence.

Alternatives to Fire

I love to smudge my home, but I like to alternate with a hydrosol spray. You can also use an essential oil diffuser as an effective way to gently clear, cleanse and fill a space.

Tea Tree (Melaleuca alternifolia)

Natural antiseptic and fungicide that can be used irectly on the skin. Apply to wounds, burns, and insect bites. Important in any natural first-aid kit.

#1 ASKED QUESTION

How Long Will My Recipe Last?

This is one of the most common questions and one of the hardest to answer. Here are a few rules for getting the longest life out of your recipe.

Make Small Batches

-Most recipes only take a few minutes to mix up, so it's better to start small and remake often rather than having it spoil.

Enjoy it Fresh

-Recipes with fresh ingredients should be used immediately. You can keep them in the fridge, but they probably won't last more than a week.

Store it Properly

-Keep your homemade beauty products in airtight containers in a cool, dry spot. Consider refrigerating your creations, which can extend their shelf life.

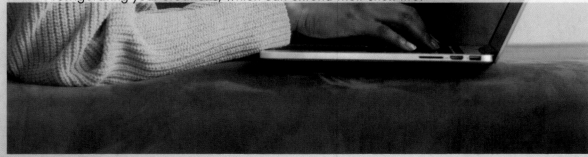

SEASON BY SEASON INDEX

Spring

Summer

SEASON BY SEASON INDEX

Acknowledgments

I am so grateful to everyone who made this book possible. First and foremost, to the generations, past, present, and future healers from Africa to the Americas, who have carried, carry, and will continue to carry on our rich connections to family, community and land. I give thanks for the gift of the ancestral connection with my brother, Michael Gilmore, that refills my cup and faith in people during this time of evolution.

Thank you to my incredible family: all of my aunts, uncles, cousins, nieces, and my nephew for giving me the inspiration to share my stories. I would like to thank my parents, Patricia and Edward, for their love, support and for sharing their childhood stories with me. The many hours of retelling family memories are priceless to me.

To Aunt Cynthia, for your continued love, support and for helping to organize my life so that I could finish this book with my sanity intact. To my cousins, Takiyah and Jamilah, for being constant supporters and champions in everything that I do. Your steadfast courage and tenacity for life continues to inspire me. To my sister, Courtney, thank you for being my pinky conspirator and a mirror of sweetness, love, strength, and faith.

Thank you to my teachers Siri Rishi Kaur and Karen Rose for their steady presence, heart lead guidance, and wisdom over the years.

Hi, I'm Conya

Conya Gilmore is the founder of
Rising Rooted Apothecary and
Virginia based Herbalist. She is a
graduate of Howard University and
Sacred Vibes Apothecary Herbal
Apprenticeship.

Conya teaches and lives in Virginia
with her family.

RISING ROOTED APOTHECARY
PLANT BASED BEAUTY BOOK

thank you!

WANT TO LEARN MORE?
WWW.RISINGWHILEROOTED.COM